THE TEMPORAL ENGINEERING™ OF SOFTWARE

ROBOT ARM AND ETL DATA MIGRATION

GORDON MORRISON

outskirts press

Dedicated to

M Catherine Morrison — confident, courageous, intelligent, independent, and self-sufficient. Thank you for your encouragement and understanding while I put this second book together.

And

Ron Riedesel, a wonderful friend who brightened many of my days, and who was lost to all of us in the spring of 2008. Remembered always.

The following are reviews of this technology:

"This technique is so powerful and adaptive that it has the potential to be developed into a complete, model-driven architecture and holds the possibility of eliminating programmers as we know them."

Dr. Aynur Anul, Silicon Valley

The thing that keeps me motivated on your approach is that I believe technology reaches perfection as it emulates the divine Creator's works. Since COSA works more like the human brain than the Touring model or John von Neumann's architecture, it is no doubt a better approach.

Gregory M. Pope
Software Quality Engineering Group Leader/Science and Technology Center
SQE Project Lead/Advanced Simulation Computing V&V
Lawrence Livermore National Laboratory

COSA is spot on . . . I have finished reading your book "Breaking the Time Barrier." I found your analysis of the problem and proposed solution spot on. Your logic is impeccable. The biggest problem today with software (besides its ever-increasing complexity) is incomplete logic. That incomplete logic is directly attributable to the ITE style of coding. For example, consider the following pseudo code:

If (1 = buffer_size = 1000) Then (++buffer_size)
do something

The flaw in this logic is that there is no error handling when the buffer size is greater than 1000. The buffer size counter won't be incremented but the "do something" code will still be executed. A simplistic example, yes. But similar coding mistakes have led to buffer overflow and other security exploits in commercially available software.

You sum it up well on page 8: "Because most COSA tables represent binary behavior, errors in logic and operation are covered by default. This is not true in the traditional ITE approach, which requires the programmer to define a contrary action." This is the key "selling point" of this methodology.

I particularly like the embedded trace capability of COSA/BNF table. With typical programming techniques, the trace code has to be added and then compiled in/out. This actually creates different execution paths and timing with the trace on or off. Debugging time critical software becomes much more difficult in that case.

Another compelling argument for your proposed methodology is the elegance and simplicity of both the state and call diagrams. I think the examples you used had a 3-4x reduction compared to ITE counterparts. I have seen too many examples in actual coding where it is almost impossible to determine what is going on in the software because these diagrams are too complicated to understand.

Thanks again for the book. I enjoyed reading it.

John Terzakis, Staff Engineer/Project Manager, Intel

How can COSA provide substantial benefits for programming teams involved in embedded system development having short time to delivery and low budget constraints?

The reason that I pose this question in particular is that COSA is so different and innovative than existing PC-based programming methodologies that programmers might be overwhelmed with the change crossing the border in adopting COSA. COSA strikes right in the belly one of the most fundamental axioms of programming, namely IF-THEN-ELSE statements, which programmers feel the most comfortable with, but at the same time inadvertently open their programs to vulnerabilities, debugging cycles and spending time in unnecessary remediating measures. If they could only have developed in COSA to start with, they would have remained in time and budget control. Why? Because COSA offers better scalability and higher code quality through a more disciplined programming structure. COSA offers a simpler, safer and more economical path to complete the task; it reduces errors and complexity at source.

Nobody gets fired because he did not use a new innovative method, even if it promises such great time and costs saving benefits as COSA. So, who could be the first ones to start betting their cards on COSA?

These can be new entrepreneurs, managers and programmers of new embedded system projects, having no programming legacy or tools behind, but only limited time and budget to accomplish their new product development. COSA can come to the rescue of these new projects, allowing developing programs within one third of the time, one fourth of the number of code lines, a fraction of required memory and processing capacity to run on, using tools that are CPU vendor independent, readable by non-programmers, fully traceable, easier to debug and hence producing higher quality code than any other existing alternative.

For new project managers that must develop new embedded products fast and efficiently, and compete against established solutions in the market, COSA is the right solution to consider. Those product managers who are left with no choice, short time to market, limited or no budget – they should try COSA.

I believe that it is only a matter of time until more programmers join COSA programming to realize that the benefits outweigh tenfold the risk they had initially taken.

Uri Levy, Business Development and Marketing Technology Consultant

COSA provides the answer...,

In 20 years of software development and testing, I have sought a methodical approach to the task. With an ingrained hatred of spaghetti code, I struggled on the fringe to bring together something similar to COSA. Morrison's *Breaking the Time Barrier* outlines a cohesive and disciplined approach that has been lacking in the software industry for decades. I am pleased to see it presented in a text, which is easy to read and provides ample examples. With a strong PASCAL and Delphi experience the book resonates with me and I hope the reader unfamiliar with PASCAL and Delphi takes the time to appreciate the approach. The benefit of built in debugging will likely save time and money on many projects. I am looking forward for an opportunity to experiment with the technique and recommend the read to anyone involved in the software industry.

T. Wickard, Director of Engineering, Souriau

Gordon Morrison has used expert knowledge of compiler design techniques and data structures to produce a beautifully elegant method to write computer programs. His book is intriguing and hard to put down once started. He shows how software is simplified when control and data are fully separated. He demonstrates the clarity of logic when conditions of data are removed from the implementation. This forces the programmer to think about the logic of the solution instead of special exceptions. And he proves that programs so written are more efficient than modern programming alternatives and are, in fact, specifications with 100% traceability and observability. I found myself thinking how straightforward implementing the control solution in programmable logic would be while the data half would easily be handled in external RAM. The concepts Gordon Morrison explains will surely become commonplace.

In case you need credentials, I am a senior member of the IEEE, hold multiple engineering degrees, and hold several patents. My current title is Director of Global Technical Marketing for Premier Farnell. I was previously a Senior Engineering Manager at Harris Corporation.

Randall Restle, Director, Global Technical Marketing at Premier Farnell

I am about half-way through and I am really engaged in the approach. I suppose I may connect since it is a philosophy I share and never have seen it articulated as you have. I plan to recommend to some IT folks I know at Penn and also a couple other Dickinson alum's doing programming.

Tim Wickard, Dir of Engineering, Souriau

The book and your concept are good. I now understand the entirety of COSA. I am intrigued what a compiler written in it would look like. I am also curious about its application as an embedded platform including handling multiple interrupts and such - an engine as a thread manager.

Further, I'm interested to know what the simplest HW is required to run it. That is, if the target was a RISC processor, like a JVM except for COSA, how many instructions would it have?

I think the next challenge is to teach the approach. Perhaps, you can write and license a college course on COSA.

That COSA depends on a language that is also used to produce spaghetti code makes me wonder how to eliminate the underlying language. Having created an original computer language and written its compiler for my master's degree, I think a tool is needed and feasible that makes writing production sets a natural and direct process along with generating the corresponding tables.

Randall Restle, Director, Global Technical Marketing Premier Farnell

I read your book you gave me at the Better Software conference. I thoroughly agree with its premise.

Kenneth Pugh, Jolt Award Author Agile Development Processes
k.pugh@pughkilleen.com

Through my company I'm promoting a better approach to software development using the temporal engineering of software. It's not easy because management is generally

afraid of anything new, especially when it's promoted as being able to really help out, but it requires discipline from the developers.

I was an invited speaker at the Systems & Software Technology Conference, April 2010. The theme of the conference was "Technology: Changing the Game".

> From **www.sstc-online.org** "This year, the Systems and Software Technology Conference will explore various technologies which are expected to make abrupt changes to common thought. We will explore the tools, the processes, and the ideas which will "change the game" and make the way we have done things in the past - obsolete."

Here it is 2019 and "change the game" is still a shiny object dangling just out of reach for most.

Contents at a Glance

Preface

If you like academic works, avoid this book. I am an inventor. If you like writing and debugging if-then-else code (spaghetti code), avoid this book. That is what I am trying to get rid of. If you do not like spaghetti code, read on, learn of a cure to the common ailments that create spaghetti code.

Computer Aided Software Engineering (CASE) tools have failed in their design to eliminate spaghetti code. This design failure has resulted in CASE tools not making a solid connection between the model and the application. Until spaghetti code can be eliminated, CASE tools will remain underutilized. When approaches like CASE fail, the industry invents a new acronym and continues looking for a solution that will work. One of the new acronyms is MDA® (Model Driven Architecture). MDA is the new approach to computer-aided software engineering. Regardless of its name, MDA shares the same fundamental problem of containing spaghetti code.

What will it take to make MDA work efficiently where others have failed? The answer is, the elimination of spaghetti code. Spaghetti code can be eliminated by managing the temporal component of software development and by keeping the control-flow separate from the data-flow. This approach allows the logic to be represented in a graphical display and to associate each logical transition with a behavior to manipulate data. A well-managed temporal component eliminates the problems caused by spaghetti code. Eliminating spaghetti code would cause CASE tools to manufacture code that can stay synchronized within the model. This book is the genesis of a revolution in temporal engineering and the decline of spatial theocracy.

The differences between temporal and spatial code can be understood using another form of architecture. If the architecture of an application is viewed as a skyscraper, the members, functions, or procedures are the offices. If a skyscraper were built with a spatial architecture, there would be no hallways or elevators. The path to an office would go through connecting offices; access to different floors would be through stairs connecting directly to an office on a different floor. A trace of the spatial paths visiting the offices would look like a pile of spaghetti.

A skyscraper built with a temporal architecture will have central elevators and hallways to provide direct access to offices throughout the building without traipsing through other offices. A trace of the temporal paths visiting the offices will look like the layout of the hallways and elevators.

As the title of the book suggests, this book is about the process of Temporal Engineering™ software. This is NOT the process currently called software engineering, which is primarily an administrative process and Spatial Engineering™. To an engineer temporal software is a skill and discipline that can be repeated over and over. It is based on knowledge gained from proper mentoring and repeated reviews of one's skills. Temporal software is coherent from beginning to end and is so coherent that the model *is* the application.

Temporal Engineering of software is a disruptive technology[1] because it greatly reduces size, complexity, and thereby cost. With the cost to develop software at $10 to $100+ per line of code, reducing application size and complexity is extremely important to the corporate bottom line. When a temporal architecture is fully implemented it can reduce the size of applications up to 50%, reduce complexity by a factor of up to three times, and yet maintains the same functions and features.

As of 2018 the Department of Commerce has not updated the following report. According to a report[2] produced in the Department of Commerce software sales reached about $180 billion in 2000 with a development staff of 697,000 software engineers and an additional 585,000 computer programmers producing ITE spaghetti code. According to the same report the bugs in this annual production of software cost the US economy an estimated $60 billion. The math is easy, it is time for a new approach to software development.

The following is from US Air Force – Weapons Systems Software Management Guidebook.

---

[1] Moore, Geoffrey A., *Crossing the Chasm*, HarperCollins Publishers, 1999.
[2] Gregory Tassey, "The Economic Impacts of Inadequate Infrastructure for Software Testing", May 2002, National Institute of Standards and Technology.

2.1.7 Lack of Effective Management and Insight into Software Development

It is difficult to manage software with the same rigor as other products, since the relationship of a—completed requirements document, a top-level design, etc. to a completed working software component is not obvious. It is typical for software status to appear normal or on-schedule for long periods of time and _then change overnight_ as an important milestone approach. The late notice may be due to inadequate progress metrics, misinterpretation of what the metrics portrayed, or an unanticipated failure.

> **The bottom line is that the search for truly predictive software metrics has been elusive and achieving dependable insight into software status requires continuous attention, even when the development appears to be going well.**

Unfortunately, many of the issues noted above are all too familiar in weapon system programs. Dr. Barry Boehm, developer of the Constructive Cost Model (COCOMO) for software estimating, and author of several software development textbooks and papers, states that —Poor management can increase software costs more rapidly than any other factor. The good news is, as weapon system acquirers, Air Force program office personnel can have a significant influence on how software for weapon systems is managed. The guidance that follows is intended to directly address these critical issues.

I contend that Temporal Engineering will solve a significant number of the issues throughout the world of software because of the simplification, architecture, and trace capability from beginning to end.

About the Author

Gordon Morrison is an inventor and a consultant. He has developed real-time weather radar systems, invented the technology known today as Multi-Core and Hyper-Threading technology (U.S. Patent 4,847,755), developed extensive database systems, developed high-performance communications systems, and developed micro-code for animation. Gordon's main interest has been improving the quality of software and reducing complexity.

This book has more extensive examples of Temporal Engineering:

There are additional examples, documents, and information on my web sites at:

<u>www.VSMerlot.com</u>. AND <u>www.Purposeful-Innovation.com</u>

I have kept the basic chapters explaining the fundaments of Temporal Engineering using the five-function calculator as the example providing more detail and correcting some of the formation. All new starting at Chapter 9 – Robot Arm Logic – in 3D, Chapter 10 – Data Migration, Chapter 11 – The ETL User Interface, and Chapter 12 – Access to the Source Schema, Chapter 13 – Examining the Source Data, Chapter 14 – Accessing the Destination Schema, Chapter 15 – The Mapping State Machine, Chapter 16 – Extracting, Translating, and Loading

Before I authored this book, I was promoting the temporal approach to companies that would invite me to come and speak. I spoke at Lockheed-Martin Advance Technology Laboratory and Stanford Research I International and received warm reviews, but people said it was just too easy to mindlessly hack out code. I agree that it is too easy to hack out code. When I am exploring different approaches to some logic I will, on rare occasions, hack out the code. But when I am ready for my final logic, I convert the hack to temporal engineering. I do not like the look of hacked code and I certainly would not show any pride in some of the hacked code that I have produced over the years.

After the book came out, I was a speaker at the 2010 Software and Systems Technology Conference (SSTC-Online.org), I did a www.theDACS.com webinar and a CODE Rage 2010 webinar for Embarcadero Technologies. Slowly, like most technologies, people are beginning to move toward this temporal approach. As I point out in my reference to the poem "The Calf Path" change is very slow.

Acknowledgments

My life has been enriched with the conversations of many intelligent people. In so many ways they have guided me down this path. In countless hours of technical conversations, they have helped me through this process. Many thanks to: Fred Inman, Dick Pankoski, Robert Wilhelm, Fred Gluck, Chris Brooks, Mike Bottomley, Bret Bowman, Jan Hauser, Dave Merritt, Dr. Aynur Anul, and Dr. Richard Balay. In addition, I have enjoyed my long relationship with IEEE *Computer* magazine for giving me a good background and for not solving the problems that I have enjoyed solving.

I would like to single out three people who have special skills that were beneficial to me: Dick Pankoski for his ability to organize my rambling thoughts early in my career, and Fred Inman and Robert Wilhelm for allowing and encouraging me to be creative.

I would like to thank Scott Kosta and Mike Steward for the many hours of great conversations on previous projects that helped me realize that I needed to do a second book and push this technology on the unwilling masses.

I would like to thank Ann-Marie Scarborough for helping with the editing of this document.

For the Second Book

Thanks to all the pioneers for buying this book. Thanks for having the courage to move software development into the time domain.

CHAPTER 1
The Problem

After talking to and corresponding with many people after the first book I found that a few people have judged this book to be about a state machine. I applaud when people can simplify complex topics into something that works for them. But this book is about a new paradigm that starts with the specification in a logical engineering approach that will produce state logic for a state engine. When I have asked people to show me a state machine what they inevitability show me is a bunch of if-then-else logic which if you have heard me speak or read any of my writing, you will know I call that ITE or spaghetti code. As you read this book you will find that I am able to eliminate all but one if statement from my examples because I have separated the logic from the data manipulation.

There are several material considerations missing from the practice of software engineering. For Software Development to be an engineering profession, we need a reproducible discipline[3] with the artistry refocused to a more useful place. The creativity is in the solution, not the use of the language. Software engineering needs a better way to test, trace, and debug software. Furthermore, it needs a clearly understood temporal component[4], and a robust ability to handle misuse with a high level of confidence. This book puts forth a solution to all these needs. This is a simple solution that may initially be difficult to understand since it represents a substantial change[5] in thinking.

Seasoned computer science professionals understand why Dr. Brooks wrote about the lack of discipline in the software profession and Dr. Lee wrote about the temporal needs in software development. These individual papers are elegant proof of how intensely

---

[3] Brooks, Frederick P. Jr., "Three Great Challenges for Half-Century Old Computer Science" – *Journal of the ACM*, Vol 50 No. 1 January 2003, pp 25-26.
[4] Lee, Edward A., "Absolutely Positively on Time," *IEEE Computer*, Editorial March 8, 2005.
[5] Ernst von Glaserfeld, "The Reluctance to Change a Way of Thinking*", Irish Journal of Psychology, 1988.

the computer science profession embodies the "cobbler's children" cliché. Both distinguished professors lament about the lack of discipline in an engineering science run by young artists. A lack of discipline has resulted in software managers unable to control projects[6].

A way of solving the discipline problem is to eliminate the programmer as art and create an art in solving problems. This can be done using a Model Driven Architecture (MDA®) to manufacture the application code. However, the MDA[7] approach has failed because of a lack of continuity between the model and the implementation, causing the process to be incoherent. "Often, once construction begins, the teams leave the model behind and never update it to reflect their changing conceptions of the project."[8] The current MDA approach has failed because it doesn't solve the fundamental problem of "spaghetti code" which in turn doesn't match any model. It is extremely problematic to model free-form language. And free-form language creates an unstable application that is costly to maintain. When an application's call-logic is modeled, and the free-form code is examined, it looks like a "pile of spaghetti" (see Appendix F).

Brooks' concerns and Lee's temporal request can both be met by keeping control-flow and data-flow sections separate. This orthogonal approach results in strongly specialized functional sections. This orthogonal section makes it *impossible* to create "spaghetti code" but doesn't prevent the creation of "spaghetti logic". Even bad logic is easier to debug when it has been separated from data manipulation. In a profession not known for its discipline, this will be a challenge, but it can be accomplished through the approach shown here. A principle assumption is that the reader has an advanced understanding of the "if-then-else" (ITE) constructs of traditional code. The ITE approach imbeds the manipulation of data with the logic. For example, the construct:

"(if a <> x) then (a = a + 1); else (a = a − 1);"

contains two control-flow paths and two data-flow paths combined. The Coherent Object System Architecture (COSA) approach to coding does not allow this

---

[6] Charette, Robert N., "Why software fails. We waste billions of dollars each year on entirely preventable mistakes," © 2005 *IEEE Computer*, September 2005, page 42.
[7] MDA is a Registered Trademark of the Object Management Group, www.omg.org/mda/
[8] Mesevery, Thomas, Fenstemacher, Kurt, "Transforming Software Development: An MDA Road Map," © 2005 *IEEE Computer*, September 2005, page 52.

combination to happen.

The Software Engineering Institute (SEI) of Carnegie Mellon University (CMU) used a state machine technology to produce a successful software engineering administrative process[9]. Having a known name helps market their process Team Software Process (TSP). But, the CMU-SEI Personal Software Process (PSP) lacks the thoroughness needed to create engineered software. The PSP uses throwaway state tables that produce non-orthogonal code, which takes us right back to an ITE approach, which results in undisciplined "spaghetti code". I will show you how to keep those state tables and make them a part of your engineered product.

The TSP and PSP processes are successful given their limited use, however, the administration and engineering are faulty due to a lack of coherence. The SEI website (http://www.sei.cmu.edu) shows an example of their state template (it looks like a spreadsheet form), which gets filled in by the analyst and eventually "discarded" as documentation that will get out of sync with the application.

1.1 Summary

Before you continue please set aside your current views of logic, state machines, and the if-then-else style of producing code. You can always go back to your previous styles of developing software products if you see no value in what I provide herein.

---

[9] "Personal Software Process/Team Software Process," Sponsored by U.S. Department of Defense – © 2005 by CMU.

Chapter 2

The COSA Solution – Temporal Engineering™

This book demonstrates COSA Temporal Engineered software. This name was developed to indicate the coherence needed to move from a model to manufactured code while maintaining synchronization. The architectural structure presented in this book will transform the way problems and specifications are viewed. It will require a substantial change in thinking and discipline to avoid reverting to a Spatial Engineering™ approach.

One of the many examples of how to use COSA is a five-function calculator with the operations of "+", "-", "*", "/", and "%". This example creates an application complex enough to show the fundamentals of temporal engineering. Where the control-flow in the calculator is separate from data-flow in the calculator. This approach to application development is not limited to small applications and can be applied to significantly more complex applications. In other words, it is completely scalable. The temporal component forces the analyst/engineer to fully define each state in time. This will be more easily understood when examining the logic. The Spatial Engineering (ITE) approach does not consider time as part of its analysis; it only considers order and thereby an implicit notion of time. In the COSA implementation, time is an explicit component that moves with the control-flow logic.

The CMU-SEI (PSP) process mentioned in Chapter 1 lacks the thoroughness needed to create temporal software. PSP uses throwaway state tables that produce non-orthogonal code, resulting in undisciplined "spaghetti code" which is an ITE approach. COSA, on the other hand, starts with a grammar that leads to a table. COSA *keeps and extends these state tables* and builds the application around them. There is no waste with COSA. In addition to the specification the three essential parts of COSA are the engine, a rules table, and the supporting procedures.

2.1 An Overview of the COSA Engine

In his book, *Code Complete 2*, Steve McConnell[10] has an entire chapter on table-driven methods. He encourages the use of table-driven methods for reducing the complexity of processing data. COSA expands on the initial table-driven approach to focus on reducing the complexity of logic.

COSA is based on an engine paradigm that uses time to reduce complexity through control-flow rules in a table that contains pointers to data-flow procedures. The complexity does not go away as the result of *magic*. The complexity is replaced with temporal logic managed by the engine.

The engine consists of the following:

0 Interface Name (Attributes if any)
1 Engine Control – While Scope used for preempting an object (real-time control)
2   Testing - If managing logic analysis TRUE or FALSE
3   True Trace – managing temporal flow for debugging
4   **True Behaviors**   **- actions supporting the true logic**
5   Next True Time   - temporal control on true logic
6   OR   - Then logic
7   False Trace – managing temporal flow for debugging
8   **False Behaviors**   **- actions supporting the false logic**
9   Next False Time   - temporal control on false logic
10   End of Testing Scope
11 End of Control Scope
12 Return Value if any

Line 0 is the interface to the engine; it passes information into the engine. Line 1 is the engine's local control. The local control is tested on every iteration through the engine and will preempt the engine if the local control is set to false. When control is critical, a global state can be added to the local engine control to create a global preemption. There was a time when hitting a ctrl-A could stop an application. With the development

---

[10] McConnell, Steve, *Code Complete 2*, Copyright © 2004 Microsoft Press, Chapter 18.

of spaghetti objects, as Dick Pankoski called them[11], that control is no longer available.

Line 2 of the engine is the only place in the entire application where the "if" logic is found. This line compares the incoming dynamic state with the static state in the table. If it is true, lines 3-5 are executed. If it is false, lines 7-9 are executed. The COSA engine's only function is to traverse through the logic. (When you get to Chapter 10 on the data parser, an interesting dilemma appears that begs for ITE logic to quickly solve the problem; instead, the problem is solved with COSA, a clean temporal logic.)

Trace control for true behavior is at line 3, and trace control for false behavior is at line 7. These locations in the engine-control provide two points for the developer to analyze program behavior. In a traditional ITE application, several lines of code must be added to provide a tracing scope equivalent to these two lines of code. In the ITE approach to coding, there are no central locations in the logic, as can be found in COSA. Using the COSA approach to tracing dramatically reduces the problems of turning trace on/off and any potential side effects that may occur. For those engineers involved in medical, security, or government projects this is the ultimate software trace. Trace can be dynamic or static. Dynamic trace produces runtime application information. Static trace tracks the evolution of how code changes over time.

The engine's true behavior is at line 4, and the engine's false behavior is at line 8. Both behaviors are dynamically bound to their respective columns in the control-flow logic table on each iteration of the engine. Dynamic binding creates vast amounts of flexibility limited only by one's imagination. The artistry lies solving the logic problems used in engineering software.

After a behavior has been executed, the engine retrieves the next temporal location for the true behavior at line 5 and for the false behavior at line 9. If the engine is still turned on after the respective behavior has been completed, then it is ready for its next iteration.

2.2 An Overview of the COSA Rules Table

The COSA rules are contained in the rows of a table[12]. The COSA Rules Table has a

---

[11] Personal Conversation
[11] "Agile Programming: Design to Accommodate," IEEE *Software* May/June 2005, Dave Thomas.

dual nature that is both data and code. As data, the COSA Rules Table can change. As code, these data changes can represent a logic fix or the application changing as it learns new logic. The standard binary table in COSA has true and false logic in each row.

Regardless of the type of table implementation a row represents the temporal control-flow logic for the problem in a top-down progression of time. A row in the table represents what is expected of the problem and what to do when the expected results are received. A row in the table also represents what to do when the expected result is not received.

The columns have specific relationships to the structure of the engine. Because most COSA tables represent binary behavior, errors in logic and operation are covered by default. This is not true in the traditional ITE approach, which requires the programmer to define a contrary action. By its very definition, the binary approach used by COSA is robust beyond anything that can be achieved by the ITE approach or the State Templates used by SEI.

Recall from the preface that a skyscraper designed with ITE architecture does not have elevators or hallways. To do work "Control" dispatches a "runner" on a path, in one scenario. Since paths go through connecting offices imagine the problem of communicating an error back to control. The path would have to go through all the previous offices to get back to control to correct the problem. Finally, the runner must return through a multitude of offices to the original location where the error was encountered.

The temporal skyscraper model has elevators and hallways. The runner would simply leave the room where the problem occurred, walk down the hallway to control, correct the problem, and walk back to the appropriate office and continue working.

2.3 An Overview of the COSA Procedures

The procedures, as defined by COSA, execute one action specific to a behavior. There are times when the specific action is to do nothing because the procedure is a placeholder in the logic. When the action is complete the procedures participate in setting the correct dynamic state based on one specific action, if necessary. The true and false procedures also control turning the engines on and off as needed by the logic.

2.4 An Overview of COSA Framework

Figure 2.0 shows an abstraction of a data migration application containing eight COSA objects. Each object consists of an engine, control-flow (Tables), and data-flow (Procedures).

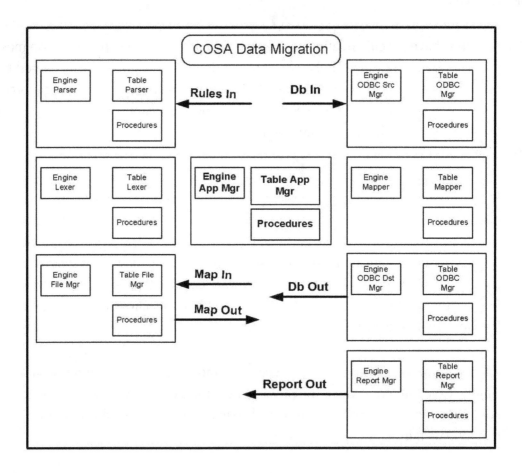

Figure 2.0
Abstraction of COSA Application

2.5 Summary

This book shows how COSA fills in the missing piece between the model and the application. The COSA approach to engineered software uses one or more engines as the pivotal point of control. The control-flow is separated from data-flow, and all the logic is in a coherent table, with simple coherent procedures. The COSA process eliminates the ITE approach that creates spaghetti code.

COSA technology is scalable. COSA works well with object technology, existing multi-threaded frameworks, or in procedural languages where embedded real-time performance, preemption, and predictability are critical.

Chapter 3

An Example Using BNF with COSA

The product we will build is a five-function calculator. We are going to put the logic of the calculator application together using a COSA Extended BNF. The application analyst put together the specification defining the product based on what the customer wants[13]. Analysts are people with experience in the business and know the specifics of what the business needs. If an analyst gave the same specification to ten equally competent software engineers, then ten distinctive designs would be received back. I have seen at least six different simple calculator designs, all work and each would be difficult to maintain because of the inherent complexity in the ITE approach. The differences in the implementation must be attributable to the interpretation of the specification. An elevated level of abstraction leaves much open for the developer to artistically create.

3.1 The Power of Using BNF

A powerful specification with a low level of abstraction can be created[14] with the use of Backus-Naur Form (BNF)[15]. The entire application can be created using a BNF structure. The Harvard Medical School in Boston started to create such a structure[16] for their internal use. It is one of many good examples of using BNF that can be found on the Internet.

It is extremely important to remember that every computer language, every Internet GUI, every database, every protocol, and every user interaction passes through a BNF filter of some sort. BNF definitions are a particularly prominent place to start any new

---

[13] The requirements are the part that constrain and cannot be implemented.
[14] The industry needs a good integrated BNF editor and development tool.
[15] Backus, John, Dec 3, 1924- Mar 17, 2007, http://en.wikipedia.org/wiki/John_Backus
[16] "BNF and built-in classes for object-oriented guideline expression language (GELLO)," © 2001 Decision Systems Group, Omolola Ogunyemi, PhD, et al. aziz@dsg.harvard.edu

application. The following is a bit of BNF humor:

> A story is told about a language processing software that could translate technical English manuals into Russian. The Russians had software that could translate technical Russian manuals into English. Both applications were exceptionally good at these technical translations. It was decided to put some prose through these language translators. On the English side they put in "*The spirit is willing, but the flesh is weak.*" And sent it to the Russians. The Russians translated the prose back into English, which resulted in "*The ghost is ready, but the meat is raw.*"

An example will provide a better understanding of how COSA works. The idea for the calculator example comes from a book by Dr. Miro Samek, *Practical Statecharts in C/C++.*[17] The COSA example produces the same functionality as the ITE five-function calculator example in Samek's book. I refer to his book because of the excellent quality and thoroughness of his work in the spatial[18] domain. I appreciate Samek's "Quantum Programming" structures for advancing state machines. However, I believe COSA presents a better way of understanding logic using a temporal domain.

According to an SEI PowerPoint[19] presentation on their licensed software process, "designed programs are smaller" and "design takes longer" to create. The next step in designing a state machine, by the SEI approach, is to fill in the State Template. This will create all the transitions among states and their respective actions taken within each state. Instead, we will take a structured language-based approach using BNF to create the logic. But this approach is not based on a fixed BNF; instead, we will be creating a dynamic BNF that will learn its domain-specific structure as the project develops.

To understand the control-flow logic in any application, a BNF approach, like the one described in this book, can be used. A BNF structure can also be used to describe and generate state diagrams, class diagrams, tree views, and a complete application. When the modeling tool maintains the underlying meta-data any change to the view represented by the tree diagram results in changes to the BNF and state diagrams.

---

[17]Samek, Miro, PhD, *Practical Statecharts in C/C++*, State Diagram on pg 170, CMP Books, © 2002.
[18] See Preface for an introduction to spatial versus temporal software.
[19] PSP II Designing and Verifying State Machines, PowerPoint Presentation, Copyright © 2005 Carnegie Mellon University.

Consistency is maintained because the traditional "code" does not exist independent from the BNF definitions. Each section in the application is represented as BNF. Each section can be viewed as the analyst prefers because the underlying BNF creates the requested view. When every aspect of the project revolves around the BNF there is no need for the insertion of comments into a language to delineate computer-generated sections from human created sections of the application.

3.2 The Calculator Specification

We are provided with a complex operating system framework within which we will be building our product. Although, we have two user approaches we can implement, the user of our product is not an engineer and does not understand stacks, so we will not be building our use case based on reverse Polish notation like HP calculators. Instead, we will be using the TI® Algebraic Operating Systems approach where the user enters a number, then an operator, then enters a second number, and then clicks an equal key to get a result.

Our user would like to be able to correct entries and clear everything. Also, our user wants to use the second operand to calculate a percent of the first operand. The user only understands simple numbers with decimal points, nothing else. The framework provided by the platform will provide the GUI and real-time interaction. We will be providing the interface to the framework and the runtime behavior.

The form of the calculator is a Windows® application with buttons that can be clicked with a mouse to create an event that results in an action or behavior. The COSA approach is to start this application with a BNF[20] definition. The operational definition for the calculator is defined as four rules: rOper1(100), rOper8(500), rOper2(700), and rResult(900). These operational rules are defined with the temporal component running from left to right and top to down. The analyst chose the trace numbers associated with each rule, and they will be used for tracking the specification throughout the development process.

The rules all start with a lower case "r". Steps will be added to the rules to complete their definitions. These individual steps will become the states within the rules. Each

---

[20] There is an international standard on Extended BNF "ISO/IEC 14977:1996(E)" called Information technology – Syntactic meta language – Extended BNF. I may or may not conform, but I will explain my usage to get my point across.

state will start with a lower case "f" for function or "i" when implemented as a constant.

$$\text{Calculator} \quad = \text{rOper1 rOper8 rOper2 rResult?};$$

In the BNF a vertical pipe "|" is used to allow for selecting between the different possibilities as in format A or format B. The less than and greater than symbols are used to contain and delineate symbol names that contain more than one word as in the unary minus. To simplify this kind of technical jargon I read these structures as "unary minus contained." As a brief reminder:

Star "*" is used to define zero or more occurrences.

Plus "+" is used to define one or more occurrences.

Question "?" denotes zero or one occurrence for an
   optional argument.

The listing 'period' 'digit' is the same as 'period' THEN 'digit'.

Vertical Pipe "|" is used as a logical choice between productions.

(When I learned BNF in college, the production assignment was delineated by "::=". This always bothered me. In a temporal sense, once an assignment has been made, all that is needed is one symbol. There can be no ambiguity. But, until now, applications have developed BNF definitions in the ITE spatial domain where the parser does not keep track of time; they only keep track of states. We will look at this further when the explicit temporal component is introduced).

The first operand needs further definition. A number is defined as a collection of one or more digits ranging from zero through nine. Numbers can exist in several forms as positive numbers "+number", or as negative numbers "-number". Numbers can also have decimal portions containing a period followed by digits. The positive number is the default representation eliminating the need for the plus sign. The *acceptable* number formats for this calculator example are defined in three productions.

The ASCII values of the characters are used in the state name. The number 59 is the value for the period (decimal point) resulting in fDot59 and is used to indicate the token's actual value when comparing the expected state to the dynamic state.

Number = fDigit+ | fDigit+ fDot59 | fDigit* fDot59 fDigit+;

It would be easy to expand on the definition of "Number" to include a production with plus or minus exponent limited to three digits {3}.

Number2 = fDigit+ fDot59 fDigit+ (e | E) (+ | -) fDigit{3};

The specification says the Number2 format is not allowed, so we will keep this production in mind for more complex applications. Each rule can easily be expanded to include "features" that were not requested. However, part of the engineering discipline is to stay as close as possible to the specification without under providing or over providing. At some point the trace numbers will be assigned to each element in the BNF and tracked back to the specification. Upon design review the trace ability of COSA will help contain "feature creep" a well-known problem in the industry.

The first operand is then defined as an optional unary minus followed by the number definition. This definition of "Number" satisfies the requirements for entering a number at rOper1 and rOper2.

rOper1 = fNeg44? Number;

The operation is defined as the four functions that can be executed on the operands using the TI calculator style called AOS.

rOper8 = fAdd43 | fSub44 | fMul42 | fDiv47;

The second operand is the same as the first operand and is defined as such.

rOper2 = rOper1;

The "Result" is more complex and is defined in terms of the percentage function and the equal sign.

The final "rResult" rule looks like the following:

rResult = fPerc37 | fEqual;

The "Number" production has been reduced[21] to the most general format used by this calculator. The complete domain specific BNF for the calculator now looks like this:

Calculator	= rOper1 rOper8 rOper2 rResult?;
rOper1 (100)	= fNeg44? Number (fClrEnt | fClear)?;
Number	= fDigit* (fDot59 fDigit+)?;
rOper8 (500)	= fAdd43 | fSub44 | fMul42 | fDiv47;
rOper2 (700)	= rOper1;
rResult (900)	= fPerc37 | fEqual;

BNF 3.0
COSA Calculator

Implicit in the BNF definition is time. Time flows from left to right and is connected through all the rules. The explicit time component will be added later.

3.3 The Calculator Look and Feel

The calculator form is designed by dragging and dropping the various components from the Delphi Toolbar.

Figure 3.0
Calculator Form

Figure 3.1
Trace Logic Listbox

---

[21] Chapter 9 covers the advanced topics of "behavior reduction" and "behavior coalescence".

All the labeled buttons have an associated "on-click" event. The display box in Figure 3.0 of the calculator does not have any associated click events. All the button "on-click" events call the calculator object "objCOSA" with their respective event data. The tab that says "Trace Logic" at the top contains a list box, shown in Figure 3.1, that displays trace/debug information. The above narrative, BNF, and the look and feel, complete the specification for the five-function calculator.

3.4 The Calculator Engine

The engine is the interface for the buttons' "on-click" events. The engine receives the tokenized value from each button's "on-click" event and a string containing the event type. The engine then compares the tokenized value of the dynamic state to the static state. If there is a match the true behavior is executed. If there is not a match the false behavior is executed. The engine transitions according to the rules defined in the COSA Rules Table and respective procedures. When the rule is complete the engine is turned off and returns control to the Windows Message Loop.

3.5 The Calculator Rules Table

The Calculator's logic table consists of an array. In this example there are seven columns consisting of four pointers and three values. The specification has given the Rules Table four rule-sections. Section 100 covers the rules for the first operand. Section 500 covers the rules for the operators. Section 700 covers the rules for the second operand. Section 900 covers the rules for the results. The analyst chose the section numbers in the specification and will maintain these numbers throughout the design, development, and trace debugging.

3.6 The Calculator Procedures

The procedures are defined as coherent, which means they perform one simple function. They provide state information and turn the engine on or off as required by the rules. The try/except containment for the operator execution is the most complex procedure in the calculator. In certain cases, procedures are also used to instantiate, communicate, or access other objects depending on the structure of an application.

3.7 Summary

BNF is used to describe and generate diagrams, views, and applications that conform to COSA. The structured language-based approach that results from BNF is used to describe the logic. Once a BNF specification has been created it acts as the basis for representations throughout the application. The specification and BNF definitions were created for the calculator.

With the structure of the engine, control-flow table, and data-flow procedures fixed, the only true variables in COSA are the logic and the algorithms that manipulate the data. The structure remains consistent throughout COSA, like a software chip.

Chapter 4

The COSA Rules Table in Detail

The previous chapter provided the fundamental BNF definition for the calculator. The four calculator rules were expanded into the steps necessary to perform the logic associated with the desired calculation of operating on two numbers and providing a result.

Calculator	= rOper1 rOper8 rOper2 rResult?;
rOper1 (100)	= fNeg44? Number (Clear | <Clear Entry>)?;
Number	= fDigit* (fDot59 fDigit+)?;
rOper8 (500)	= fAdd43 | fSub44 | fMul42 | fDiv47;
rOper2 (700)	= rOper1;
rResult (900)	= fPerc37 | fEqual;

BNF 4.0
COSA Calculator

To make the detailed Rules Table for the calculator, the next step is to layout the domain specific BNF in a vertical tree structure. The four rules have steps that perform the necessary true or false behaviors[22] to complete that rule.

---

[22] When referring to an individual method in the table that method will be called an action. When referring to a method in a table from the engine's perspective, such as true or false, that member will be called a behavior because it is acting in temporal concert with other methods thereby creating a rule.

Rule	State	Trace
rOper1	= fNeg44?	100
	= fDigit*	
	= fDot59?	
	= fDigit+	
	= fClEnt?	
	= fClear?;	
rOper8	= fAdd43?	500
	= fSub44?	
	= fMul42?	
	= fDiv47?;	
rOper2	= fNeg44?	700
	= fDigit*	
	= fDot59?	
	= fDigit+	
	= fClEnt ?	
	= fClear ?;	
rResult	= fPerc37?	900
	= fEqual?	
	= ferr86;	

Tree 4.0
COSA Calculator BNF

The above tree structure is still missing actions and the next temporal steps.

rOper1:

Looking at Table 4.0 below, if the state in rule "rOper1" step fNeg44 is true then we "Negate" the number. The calculator engine is turned off and control returns to the Windows Message Loop for the next behavior. If the entry is not a minus sign, the false behavior "Ignore" is executed because the negating of a number is optional. Because the negating of a number is optional the false "Ignore" behavior does not turn the calculator engine off. In either case, time moves on to the next step (rOper1+1) in our rule to see if it is a number. This is the first introduction to the power of "Ignore" in temporal logic.

Rule	State	True Action	Next	False Action	Next
rOper1	= fNeg44?	Negate		Ignore	

Time→

Table 4.0
COSA Extended BNF

If the "on-click" event in "rOper1" is a digit (Table 4.1), we add the digit to our integer portion of the number we are building and return control to the Windows Message Loop. Remaining at this step-in time until we no longer receive a digit as an action. If a digit is entered, the logic remains at this temporal step and the true action "Any_Number" continues to build the integer portion of the number. After each digit is received the true action "Any_Number" turns off the calculator engine. When a non-digit button is clicked the logic at the digit step is false and executes the false "Ignore" behavior, transitioning to the next step in time looking for a period.

Rule	State	True Action	Next	False Action	Next
rOper1	= fNeg44?	Negate	rOper1+1	Ignore	rOper1+1
Time→ +1	= fDigit*	Any_Number	rOper1+1	Ignore	rOper1+2

Table 4.1
COSA Extended BNF

If the "on-click" event is a period fDot59 the number being built becomes a floating-point number (Table 4.2). The period is added to the number string and the calculator engine is turned off by the "One_Period" action. Time transitions to the fractional part of the number, and control is returned to the Windows Message Loop. Control remains with the "Any_Number" fractional part until a non-digit is entered. Then the false "Ignore" behavior is executed, and control searches for the next step or rule.

Rule	State	True Action	Next	False Action	Next
rOper1	= fNeg44?	Negate		Ignore	
+1	= fDigit*	Any_Number		Ignore	
+2	= fDot59?	One_Period		Ignore	rOper1+4
+3	= fDigit*	Any_Number	rOper1+3	Ignore	rOper1+4
Time→ +4					

Table 4.2
COSA Extended BNF

If the entry is not a decimal point, then the transition is to the "Clear Entry" step. If "CE" is clicked, then the display is cleared, and the transition is back to the first step fNeg44 otherwise the false "Ignore" behavior is executed and the next step, "Clear", is considered (Table 4.3). If "C" is clicked, the display is cleared, and the transition is back to the first step fNeg44, otherwise the false "Ignore" behavior is executed, and time moves to the next temporal step of completing the first operand.

Rule	State	True Action	Next	False Action	Next
rOper1	= fNeg44?	Negate		Ignore	
+1	= fDigit*	Any_Number		Ignore	
+2	= fDot59?	One_Period	rOper1+3	Ignore	rOper1+4
+3	= fDigit*	Any_Number		Ignore	
+4	= fClEnt?	Clear_Entry	rOper1	Ignore	
+5	= fClear?;	Clear	rOper1	Push_Disp	rOper8
Time→					

Table 4.3
COSA Extended BNF

At this point, most of these Rule/Step transitions should be obvious. What is not obvious to the customer is the internal housekeeping that needs to be undertaken. The customer does not recognize the need of moving and saving values for further actions. As the analyst, we know that we are going to operate on two values and therefore must keep those two values throughout an appropriate state and action. In Table 4.3 the action "Push_Disp" is created to convert the first operand string to a number and save it for the anticipated calculation.

rOper8:

Now there is a number ready to operate on. Any match in "rOper8" moves time to "rOper2". For the sake of discussion, let us assume the operation "*" (multiply) was clicked. In Table 4.4, the calculator engine "Ignores" its way from the fractional portion of the first operand at step "rOper1+3", past "rOper8", and "rOper8+1", to "rOper8+2" the logic of fMul42. At this point the engine found a match between the dynamic state from the user's click and the static state in the rule. With a match at "rOper8+2" time moves to the next rule at "rOper2".

	Rule	State	True Action	Next	False Action	Next
	rOper1	= fNeg44?	Negate		Ignore	
	+1	= fDigit*	Any_Number		Ignore	
	+2	= fDot59?	One_Period		Ignore	
	+3	= fDigit*	Any_Number		Ignore	
	+4	= fClEnt?	Clear_Entry		Ignore	
	+5	= fClear?;	Clear		Push_Disp	
	rOper8	= fAdd43?	Addition		Ignore	rOper8+1
	+1	= fSub44?	Subtraction		Ignore	rOper8+2
Time→	+2	= fMul42?	Multiply	rOper2	Ignore	
	+3	= fDiv47?	Division		Ignore	rError

Table 4.4
COSA Extended BNF

rOper2:

At this time, the calculator engine has transitioned to the next rule, "rOper2", where any state, true or false, can turn off the engine. In each of the true actions, "Addition", "Subtraction", "Multiply", and "Division", a line of code could have been added to turn the engine off. In this example, the analyst chose to add a line of logic to indicate that the engine is explicitly turned off. With the action "Engine_Off", the temporal pointer has the calculator engine waiting for the next "on-click" event for the second operand to be entered.

Rule	State	True Action	Next	False Action	Next
rOper1	= fNeg44?	Negate		Ignore	
+1	= fDigit*	Any_Number		Ignore	
+2	= fDot59?	One_Period		Ignore	
+3	= fDigit*	Any_Number		Ignore	
+4	= fClEnt?	Clear_Entry		Ignore	
+5	= fClear?;	Clear		Push_Disp	
rOper8	= fAdd43?	Addition		Ignore	
+1	= fSub44?	Subtraction		Ignore	
+2	= fMul42?	Multiply		Ignore	
+3	= fDiv47?;	Division		Ignore	
rOper2	= fOff	Engine_Off	rOper2+1	Engine_Off	rOper2+1
+1					

Time→

Table 4.5
COSA Extended BNF

As we continue with "rOper2" the logic associated with the second operand is like the logic of first operand with the addition of the "Save_Disp" true or false behavior after the fClear step (Table 4.6). The "Save_Disp" action creates the second number ready for the appropriate operator action. When the second operand has been entered and "CE" or "C" have not been clicked then the "rOper2" rule transitions control to the "rResult" rule.

Rule	State	True Action	Next	False Action	Next
rOper1	= fNeg44?	Negate		Ignore	
+1	= fDigit*	Any_Number		Ignore	
+2	= fDot59?	One_Period		Ignore	
+3	= fDigit*	Any_Number		Ignore	
+4	= fClEnt?	Clear_Entry		Ignore	
+5	= fClear?	Clear		Push_Disp	
rOper8	= fAdd43?	Addition		Ignore	
+1	= fSub44?	Subtraction		Ignore	
+2	= fMul42?	Multiply		Ignore	
+3	= fDiv47?	Division		Ignore	
rOper2	= fOff	Engine_Off		Engine_Off	
+1	= fNeg44?	Negate		Ignore	
+2	= fDigit*	Any_Number		Ignore	
+3	= fDot59?	One_Period		Ignore	
+4	= fDigit*	Any_Number		Ignore	
+5	= fClEnt?	Clear_Entry	rOper2	Ignore	rOper2+6
+6	= fClear?	Clear	rOper1	Save_Disp	rResult

Table 4.6
COSA Extended BNF

rResult:

Time moves to the "rResult" rule from "rOper2" if the percent sign or the equal sign is clicked. The proper calculation is executed, the result is displayed, the temporal pointer is returned to the proper rule "rOper1", and the engine is turned off. Selecting the proper operation for the calculator is not part of the actual mechanism of the control-flow logic. The actual mechanism is to setup a generic procedure pointer to execute the operation when the equal button is selected. As such, that mechanism does not show up in the logic table. The following table shows the complete rules for the calculator as specified by the customer.

	Rule	State	True Action	Next	False Action	Next
Time→	rOper1	= fNeg44?	Negate		Ignore	
	+1	= fDigit*	Any_Number		Ignore	
	+2	= fDot59?	One_Period		Ignore	
	+3	= fDigit*	Any_Number		Ignore	
	+4	= fClEnt?	Clear_Entry		Ignore	
	+5	= fClear?	Clear		Push_Disp	
	rOper8	= fAdd43?	Addition		Ignore	
	+1	= fSub44?	Subtraction		Ignore	
	+2	= fMul42?	Multiply		Ignore	
	+3	= fDiv47?	Division		Ignore	
	rOper2	= fOff	Engine_Off		Engine_Off	
	+1	= fNeg44?	Negate		Ignore	
	+2	= fDigit*	Any_Number		Ignore	
	+3	= fDot59?	One_Period		Ignore	
	+4	= fDigit*	Any_Number		Ignore	
	+5	= fClEnt?	Clear_Entry		Ignore	
	+6	= fClear?	Clear		Save_Disp	
	rResult	= fPerc37	Percent	rOper1	Ignore	rResult+1
	+1	= fEqual	Equals	rOper1	Ignore	rResult+2
	+2	= fErr86	Error	rOper1	Error	rOper1

Table 4.7
COSA Extended BNF

The "rResult" rule completes the COSA logic for the calculator. An error-handling step has been added to the "rResult" rule. This error-handling step will be connected to the false action of the fDiv47 step in the "rOper8" rule. The next chapter on procedures provides the internal detail of the behaviors.

4.1 The COSA Extended BNF Rules Table

As a part of the ongoing review process the assigned trace numbers have stayed correlated with the customer's specification and the application's logic. The process of correlating between the specification and the implementation can result in finding feature creep, i.e. things being added that were not requested, and specification

25

completeness. This correlation process can also point out errors or weaknesses that may require additions to the specification.

The specification is repeated here to show how it correlates with the trace. The user enters a number (trace 100), the user enters an operator (trace 500), the user enters a second number (trace 700), and finally hits an equal key (trace 901) to get a result. Our user also asked to be able to correct entries (trace 104 and 705) or clear everything (trace 105 and 706).

Our user wants to use the second operand to calculate a percent (trace 900) of the first operand. The user only understands simple numbers with decimal points (trace 101-103 & 701-703), and nothing else. The user decides the calculator needs additional functionality to be useful; a feature needs to be added. The ability to chain operations (trace 902) has been authorized as an addition to the specification.

The result is now defined in terms of being able to continue additional operations allowing the chaining together of operations as one would do in summing several numbers.

fChain = rOper8 rOper2;

The fChain definition reuses the "rOper8" rule T and the second operand "rOper2" to continue calculations.

The following BNF has added brackets containing the true and false links. These links are relative to the rule they are contained in or to a specific rule. For example, the 'rAdd[rOper2,1]' indicates that if the test is true, go to "rOper2" else go to "rOper8+1".

```
Calc =      rOper1(100) rOper8(500) rOper2(700) rResult(900);
rOper1 =    fNeg44?[1,1]::ClrBuf fDigit+[1,2] (fDot59[3,4] fDigit+[4,5])?
rOper8 =    (<fClear Entry>?[rOper1,5] | fClear?[rOper1, rOper8]::Push);
rOper2 =    fAdd43[rOper2,1]  |  fSub44[rOper2,2]  |  fMul42[rOper2,3]  |
rResult =   fDiv47[rOper2,rOper2];
            fNeg44?[1,1]::ClrBuf fDigit+[1,2] (fDot59[3,4] fDigit+[4,5])?
            (<rClear Entry>?[rOper2,5]| rClear?[rOper1,rResult)::Save];
            fPerc37[rOper1,1] | fEqual[rOper1,2] | rChain[rOper8,rOper1];
```

4.1 Calc Extended BNF

The step '<rClear Entry>?' is treated as one word in the Generator creating the code as 'rClear_Entry'. This complete extended BNF file is used to generate the COSA Table, the prototype functions and procedures, and the function and procedure stubs in the code.

Table 4.8 shows the completed BNF as it was implemented with the temporal connections filled in from the reasoning process we just went through. Figure 8.4 (page 108) provides a screen shot of the 2018 Prototype COSA Matrix Generator using the Complete Extended BNF.

// // Rule	Static State	True Action	Next True Rule	False Action	Next False Rule	Trace
rOper1,	fNeg44,	Negate,	rOper1+1,	ClrBuf,	rOper1+1,	100
rOper1+1,	fDigit,	Any_Number,	rOper1+1,	Ignore,	rOper1+2,	101
rOper1+2,	fDot59,	One_Period,	rOper1+3,	Ignore,	rOper1+4,	102
rOper1+3,	fDigit,	Any_Number,	rOper1+3,	Ignore,	rOper1+4,	103
rOper1+4,	fClEnt,	Clear_Entry,	rOper1,	Ignore,	rOper1+5,	104
rOper1+5,	fClear,	Clear,	rOper1,	Push_Disp,	rOper1+6,	105
// operate						
rOper8,	fAdd43,	Addition,	rOper2,	Ignore,	rOper8+1,	500
rOper8+1,	fSub44,	Subtraction,	rOper2,	Ignore,	rOper8+2,	501
rOper8+2,	fMul42,	Multiply,	rOper2,	Ignore,	rOper8+3,	502
rOper8+3,	fDiv47,	Division,	rOper2,	Ignore,	rError,	503
// next operand						
rOper2,	fNeg44,	Negate,	rOper2+1,	ClrBuf,	rOper2+1,	700
rOper2+1,	fDigit,	Any_Number,	rOper2+2,	Ignore,	rOper2+2,	701
rOper2+2,	fDot59,	One_Period,	rOper2+4,	Ignore,	rOper2+4,	702
rOper2+3,	fDigit,	Any_Number,	rOper2+4,	Ignore,	rOper2+4,	703
rOper2+4,	fClEnt,	Clear_Entry,	rOper2+1,	Ignore,	rOper2+5,	704
rOper2+5,	fClear,	Clear,	rOper1,	Save_Disp,	rResult,	705
// equals						
rResult,	fPer37,	Percent,	rOper1,	Ignore,	rResult+1,	900
rResult+1,	fEqual,	Equals,	rOper1,	Ignore,	rResult+2,	901
rResult+2,	fChain,	Oper8,	rOper8,	Oper8,	rError,	902
rError,	fErr86,	Unknown,	rOper1,	Error,	rOper1,	993

Table 4.8
Completed COSA Extended BNF

The COSA extended BNF Rules Table uses columns to define:

1) The rule name and step
2) What is being looked for – static state
3) What to do with the item when it is found – true Action
4) What to do next after the item has been dealt with – next true rule
5) What to do if the item is not found – false Action
6) What to do next when the desired item is not found – next false rule
7) A trace of what has been done.

Furthermore, the Action columns are dynamically bound to the engine and represent *behaviors* while the individual cells in the Action columns represent the *methods* of the class. The "Negate" method is referred to as a behavior when it is executed from the engine.

4.2 Understanding COSA States

One definition of cohesion is, "Do one thing and do it well." Each row in the COSA Extended BNF Rules Table is a state; each state is a step in a rule. Each row does this one state very well. Each row provides for a true and a false behavior for the engine and a true and a false next step and trace.

Accurate documentation is an added benefit of the COSA Extended BNF Rules Table. The documentation can be shown as a spreadsheet or in tree format, expanded or collapsed. If management wants a verbal description, a narrative can be attached as a link to each row.

In contrast to how COSA states are defined, in another example of a calculator,[23] Horrocks creates eight states to describe the five-function calculator. They are numbered and labeled as:

---

[23] Horrocks, Ian, *Constructing the User Interface with Statecharts*, pp. 115-121, Addison-Wesley, 1999.

1) Start,
2) Negative Number,
3) Operand1,
4) Operator Entered,
5) Negative Number,
6) Operand2 and C,
7) Alert (message), and
8) Result.

These eight states are low in cohesion because each state will do many things. In an attempt to explain a state authors and analysts add transitional narrative to the connection (transition) arrows between the states contributing further to a low level of cohesion (Figure 4.0).

Software developers will interpret the narrative in diverse ways causing many dissimilar results. A critic might argue that these state diagrams are meant to be abstract and not part of the implementation. Each transitive narrative in Figure 4.0 is devoid of any explicit time. Without a temporal component the developer must make decisions about the software design based on professional experience. And there is conflict in Figure 4.0 between what a transitive narrative (CE) does and what a state '1' does. Clear Entry is defined as a transition while clear is defined as a state. In this situation the developer could choose to require a second operand be successfully entered before the clear can even be used.

The confusion can be seen in the 4 Operator Entered state by the loop back arrow at the top right of the state. This indicates that the user can repeatedly enter "+","+","+","+", and "+" as long as they want.

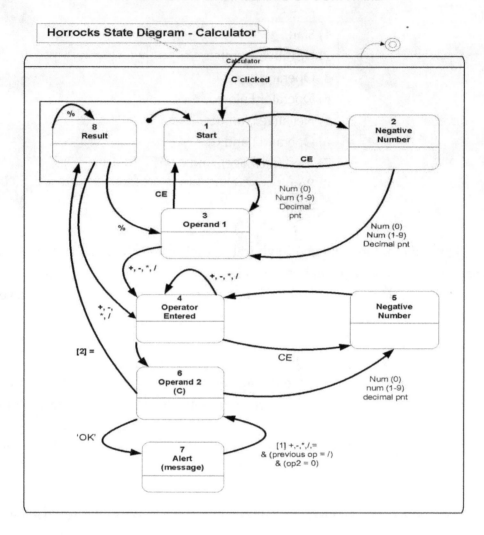

Figure 4.0
Another ITE Calculator Statechart

The logic of high abstraction is why the MDA approach continues to have problems. At some point in time (no pun intended), all the information must be present under the abstraction for MDA to succeed. The generally accepted use of highly abstract statecharts will continue to contribute to MDA not meeting its full potential.

In a different example of how states are treated the CMU-SEI "L7 State Machines.ppt" presentation[24] shows mixing data manipulation and control-flow in the same diagram.

---

[24] "Personal Software Process/Team Software Process" slide 19, Sponsored by U.S. Department of Defense – © 2005 by CMU.

Mixing reduces the cohesion of the design. The COSA Extended BNF Table does not support mixing of data manipulation because it can only represent logic.

The COSA Extended BNF Table 4.8 shown previously is a part of the model and it is the logic of the application. This makes it consistent with the state diagram because the state diagram is drawn from the BNF. The choice is to view the COSA Extended BNF Table or the Graphic Tree as in Tree 4.0 shown earlier created from the BNF. Changes to the BNF are reflected in the Graphic Tree, and changes to the Graphic Tree are reflected in the BNF. The model and application remain in sync and coherent.

All COSA states are binary and are managed by the temporal cursor iTime[25]. When a COSA state diagram is produced the states are numbered with their respective trace values. These states generally transition in chronological order. Transitioning to earlier states or repeating states forms iterative loops.

The engine definition and a couple of engine controls have been added to the BNF. The bEngine set to FALSE stops the engine and allows control to return to the Windows Message Loop. The definition of fDigit is that any single digit can be entered. Every time a digit is entered into the calculator the engine is turned off and control is returned to the Windows Message Loop to wait for the next event. This allows the calculator to build complex numbers one digit at a time.

The Push_Disp and Save_Disp are the display values being used in the calculation. The rOper1+5 fClear state keeps the first value available to be used in the subsequent operation calculation. The rOper2+5 fClear state is specific to the potential to chain operations.

The state diagram in Figure 4.1 does not need narrative labels to describe transitions to other states. Because of the elevated level of cohesion, each state has only true or false transitions. There is little room for errors in interpretation with a COSA binary state diagram.

The solid lines represent true logic and dashed lines represent false logic (when it does not matter if the result is true or false that logic is represented by a dash-dot line). The model is the application whether the model is represented as BNF, tree diagram, state

---

[25] So that the rules will fit on a single line portrait orientation, programmer-abbreviated names like "rOper8" and <iNeg44> are used.

diagram, or UML boxes-with-strings; the consistency is easy to keep.

The COSA State Diagram (Figure 4.1) is easy to understand. The inner box labeled "Oper1" contains the states that build the first operand. The inner box labeled "Oper8" contains the operators add, subtract, multiply, and divide. The inner box labeled "Oper2" contains the states that build the second operand. And the inner box labeled "Result" performs the work related to the selected operation. Anyone that can use a five-function calculator should be able to understand the flow of logic in the statechart in figure 4.1.

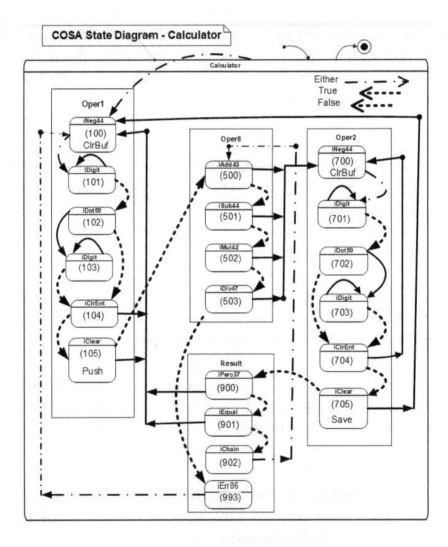

Figure 4.1
COSA State Diagram

Notice how the following domain-specific BNF 4.1 is still synchronized with the state diagram of Figure 4.1. The state diagram of Figure 4.1 is just a different representation of the COSA Extended BNF Rules Table 4.8.

Calculator	**= Calc;**
:Calc	**= Oper1 Oper8 Oper2 Result;**
Oper1(100)	**= fNeg44?[1,1]::ClrBuf Digit+[1,2] (Dot[3,4]**
	Digit+[4,5])? Clear?[Oper1,5]
	<Clear Entry>?[Oper1,Oper8]:ClrEnt:Push_Disp;
Oper8(500)	**= Add[Oper2,1]	Sub[Oper2,2]	Mul[Oper2,3] |**
	Div[Oper2,Oper2];
Oper2(700)	**= fNeg44?[1,1]::ClrBuf Digit+[1,2] (Dot[3,4]**
	Digit+[4,5])? Clear?[Oper1,5]
	<Clear Entry>?[Oper2,Result]:ClrEnt:Save_Disp;
Result(900)	**= Perc[1,1]	Equal[Oper1,2]	Chain[Oper8,Oper1];**

BNF 4.1

COSA Calculator

The rules are shown as dominate (left justified) in the column under Engine. In addition to starting with the lower case 'r', the rules make up the reference point for events in time. A step's state starts with the lower case 'i' or 'f' and become the elements within their respective rules. For example, in the generated version of the calculator the Neg44 becomes fNeg44 as a function testing if the dynamic state is a '44' returning true if there is a match. The true behavior becomes pNeg44 the 'p' indicating a procedure starting the build of the number with a '-' to create a negative number.

"rOper1, fNeg44, pNeg44, rOper1+1..."

4.3 Operational Analysis of the COSA Rules Table

The operational analysis provides a runtime understanding of the logic. The operation and the initial test of the calculator are divided into four parts:

1) Operand one is "–3.14159",
2) The operation is "–",

3) Operand two is "–2.14159", and

4) "=" Produces a result of "–1".

Using the mouse to click on the calculator-form enters each digit or decimal point into the display. Clicking on an operator will result in the display being cleared for the next operand to be entered. The trace files from both COSA and ITE approach will show the state transitions. The complete individual trace files for both applications are attached as appendices A and B.

The calculator starts in the "Run" state at trace 100 (t100). This simple calculator does not have a change sign button, so clicking on the "-" sign to negate a number can only happen before a number is entered as the first operand. Step 1) of the test starts with clicking on the minus sign to create a negative number. This is the fNeg44 state at t100.

For more detail, the "expanded" COSA state diagram in Appendix I shows the state name, e.g. fNeg44, the true behavior "Negate", and the false behavior "ClrBuf," a true next state solid arrow, and a false next state dashed arrow. (If currently these details are not import to you, continue to refer to Figure 4.1.)

Figure 4.2
COSA Calculator Form

Logically it does not matter whether the first entity is a negative sign or not. The next "iTime" transition will be the whole portion of the number being built. The temporal component keeps track of its time sequence in the operational loop eliminating the need for any ambiguous group of flags or variables. If the state is negative the working buffer is cleared by ClrBuf. Whether the state is true or false, there is only one temporal target for leaving the fNeg44 state: the fDigit state t101.

Continuing our test, the number 3 button is clicked, and the next "iTime" remains at fDigit state at t101. Figure 4.0 shows the fDigit state at t101 repeating, this happens until the button clicked on the calculator is not a number.

The period button is clicked, and "iTime" transitions to the fDot59 state at t102. Like the fNeg44 state at t100, the fDot59 state at t102 can only transition to the next state, fDigit state t103. Since only one period is allowed in a valid number, the transition must be to another "iTime". As the fractional portion of the number is entered, "14159", the "iTime" iterates on the fDigit state at t103 until the button clicked is not a number.

Step 2) An operation button is clicked, the subtract in this example, and "iTime" transitions through fClEnt state at t104 as false, through fClear state at t105 as false, through fPush state at t106 as false, through the fAdd43 state at t500 as false, and finally to the fSub44 subtraction state at t501 as true. The true operation rule sends the next "iTime" to fOff at t700 skipping the other operator states at t502 and t503. State fOff turns the engine off sending control back to the Windows Message Loop to wait for the next button click.

After an operation has been entered and before the second operand is entered, the unary minus can be entered for the second operand. The trace files, in Appendix A & B, compare COSA at step 17 to the ITE approach at a range from step 55 to step 61.

Step 3) The operation and second operand look like this "- - 2.14159" with back-to-back button clicks on the negative, one for the operation and one for the unary minus. "iTime" transitions to fNeg44 state at t701, followed by fDigit state at t702, then the fDot59 state at t703, and finally the fDigit state at t704. The temporal connections are comparable to the first operand. The behaviors are the same since the first operand was pushed internally using "Push_Disp" for the calculation coming up.

Step 4) At this stage the equal sign "=" is clicked to create a result. "iTime" transitions to fClEnt state at t705 as false, fClear state at t706 as false, then to fSave state at t707 as false. The next state checked is fPerc37 state at t900 as false, then to fEqual state at t901 as true, producing the result.

Seventeen state events were entered for this calculation example. Doing the same calculation, the complete COSA trace shows 20 state transitions (Appendix A), as compared to the 95 state transitions in the complete ITE trace (Appendix B). More than 4.75 times the number of states must be transitioned to do the work using traditional "if-then-else" logic.

4.4 The ITE State Diagram View

The contents of the COSA Extended BNF Table can clearly be seen in the COSA state diagram in Figure 4.1. Since each row in the COSA Extended BNF Table 4.8 has two possible state transitions and, as would be expected, the state diagram also has two possible transitions to the next state: true or false. The predictability of this binary state design greatly simplifies the transition logic compared to the multiple state transitions in the ITE traditional approach shown in Figure 4.3.

The ITE Statechart shows three transitions out of the "ready" (1) state, four transitions from the "negated1" (3) state, and five transitions into the "opEntered" (8) state. The temporal component is missing in the state diagram of Figure 4.3. Comparing the trace files for the two applications the simplification produced by COSA can be seen. When both applications enter "-3.14159" the progress is at count number 9 in the COSA trace file (Appendix A), as compared to count number 47 in the ITE trace file (Appendix B).

There has been a significant amount written[26] about the extremely perplexing task of verifying software. The reduction in complexity along with the increased trace coverage provided by a COSA implementation can make this "Grand Challenge" quite manageable when compared to ITE.

The following statement about the ITE State Diagram in Figure 4.3 makes it clear why we have so many problems with software correctness and verification. As Samek points out:

---

[26] "First Steps in the Verified Software Grand Challenge", *IEEE Computer Society*, Jim Woodcock, October 2006

"Arriving at this Statechart was definitely not trivial, and you shouldn't worry if you don't fully understand it at the first reading (I wouldn't either)."[27]

Not only is this Statechart in Figure 4.3 "not trivial to understand", it is equally not trivial to program and any software engineer should worry about its implementation.

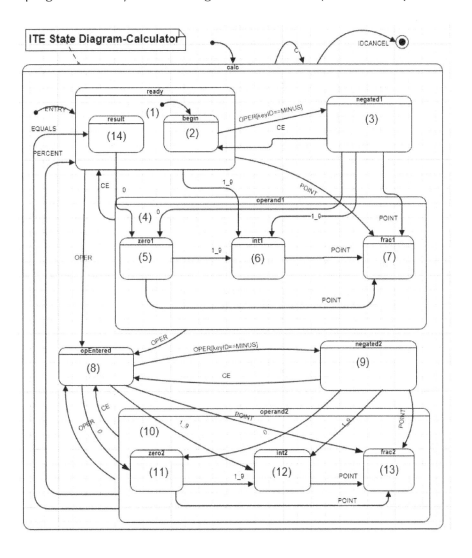

Figure 4.3
ITE Calculator Statechart

---

[27] Samek, Miro, PhD, *Practical Statecharts in C/C++*, page 8, section 1.2.2, CPM Books © 2002.

Statecharts should make understanding the solution easier, and they should be highly cohesive defining one state and doing it very well. This rule should never be broken.

4.5 Summary

This chapter covered the correlation of the specification with the BNF, which then led to the creation of a tree that then produced the COSA Extended BNF Table. Each of these steps represents different refined views of the same information.

In the process of building the COSA Extended BNF Table the static states represent what is expected at each step-in time. This approach results in a quite simple and easy to understand statechart that is unambiguous because each step-in time can only produce a true or false result.

In the traditional ITE approach without an understanding of time, flags *must* be set throughout the application to indicate in which mode the application is at any given time. The ITE state machine approach results in a very complex statechart[28]. Designers, modelers, and authors put forth statecharts with labeled arrows between states. These labeled arrows create an ambiguous[29] meaning because they are open to interpretation.

---

[28] Samek, Miro, *Practical Statecharts in C/C++,* 2002 CMP Books, page 8.
[29] US Air Force – Weapons Systems Software Management Guidebook. READ SECTION – 2.1.7 Lack of Effective Management and Insight into Software Development

Chapter 5

The COSA Engine in Detail

COSA uses three structures to develop the objects that make up an application: engine, control-flow table, and data-flow methods. The engine is a single point of control that time-manages the running of an object. The control-flow table contains the rules associated with the object and determines the object's runtime logical behavior. The data-flow methods (procedures) use no arguments since they should only be called from within the object controlled by the engine and the control-flow table. The only entry into the object should be through the engine and the interfaces it defines. This makes for a very nice "black-box" software chip design.

```
procedure TCOSAcalc.Run(intState : integer; sNumber : String);
2  begin
3        engLocal := TRUE;
4        dynamicState := intState;
5        sArgValue := sNumber;
6        while (engLocal) AND (engGlobal) do
7        begin
8                if rRule[iTime].fState then
9                begin
10                       rRule[iTime].pTrueRule;        // Dynamically True Behavior
11                       True_Trace(iTime);             // TRUE TRACE GREEN
12                       iTime := rRule[iTime].iTrueRule; // Next True Rule Time
13               end else
14               begin
15                       rRule[iTime].pFalseRule;       // Dynamically False Behavior
16                       False_Trace(iTime);            // FALSE TRACE RED
17                       iTime := rRule[iTime].iFalseRule; // Next False Rule Time
18               end;
19        formCalc.editdisplay.Text := sBuildNumber;
20 end;
```

Code Segment 5.0
Delphi COSA Calculator Engine

The engine is preempted by a false condition on line 6, with the engine's "while" statement. The local control and global control are designed into the overall application to handle its runtime execution. If either the global control or local control are false, the engine will cease execution. No matter how many objects have been instantiated below a COSA object, they can be terminated quickly with the global control, provided that a procedure does not contain an infinite loop.

The importance of the "while" statement cannot be overstated; it provides the single point of control and the ability to preempt after each iteration of the instantiated object. An application's designer should always take this fact into consideration. Behaviors that are complex and take a long time to return control to the engine circumvent this important architectural feature.

In the calculator example the local engine state "engLocal" is the control for running the engine within the object. The engine state "engGlobal" allows for global control to terminate the object separately from the local control. Monitoring the global engine state, with a high priority thread, can control graceful and emergency shutdowns. Other engine states can be joined in conjunction for control scenarios that are beyond this introduction.

The trace mechanism is built into the engine as an inherent part of COSA. Trace covers 100% of the logic because it is centralized in the engine. There can be two trace methods, one for the true behavior and one for the false behavior. Using two different trace methods allows for differing levels of detail on the true and false behaviors. Alternatively, there can be a single trace where the argument is signed to indicate true or false behaviors. Either way, trace can be as robust as desired to cover the logic and data manipulation. The procedure calls to the trace routines are at lines 11 and 16 in this Delphi implementation of the COSA engine.

5.1 Centralized Control of Runtime

The dynamic state is passed into the engine by the object's interface and is passed to the "if" statement of line 8. This is the only "if" statement in each COSA Engine. The origin of the dynamic state for this application is from the "on-click" message logic of Windows. The "if" compares the dynamic state to the static state of the current (iTime) temporal rule or step within the control-flow logic.

The dynamic binding statements at lines 10 and 15 are very technically complex. The COSA dynamic binding statements provide a consistent way to include both "Polymorphism and Dynamic Binding" into an engineered[30] approach.

5.2 Polymorphism and Dynamic Binding

"Polymorphism and dynamic binding offer a first step to developing software that runs in an open world. As an example, suppose that an application is initially designed to deal with a certain device, such as a fax machine. Through a variable f of class Fax, you can send a fax by writing f.sendFax(t,n), where t is a text and n is a fax number.

Suppose that you later add to the system a new device, such as a fax with phone, which provides its own way of sending faxes. If FaxWithPhone is a derived class of Fax, which redefines operation sendFax, variable f can refer to it, and the result of f.sendFax(t,n) would result in sending the fax using the redefined method of class FaxWithPhone. More important, the client component that uses variable f to send faxes isn't affected by the change.

The compiler checks for correctness by assuming that f's type is defined by class Fax, but the invocation of sendFax is ensured to be correct even if the dynamic type of the object referred by f is FaxWithPhone. Indeed, the client continues to work correctly with the newly defined device as it did earlier.

This simple example shows that the flexibility that polymorphism and dynamic binding provide can coexist with the discipline and safety that strong typing supports." [31]

What Thomas is referring to in his *IEEE* article is replacing an old object (Fax) with a new object (FaxWithPhone) and the new device works just like the old one. But what about the new features provided by the new device? Polymorphism alone does not allow new features to be dynamically bound with the new device without replacing the parent or calling object. COSA provides more than polymorphism. The combination of the COSA engine and the COSA Extended BNF Table provide an environment where the table can be used to *learn* new behaviors by dynamically changing the rules. The parent object that called the old object (Fax) and the new object (FaxWithPhone) can have new rules added to handle the new features. Suppose that the FaxWithPhone new feature is to redial "n" times when a busy line is detected. The parent object does not

---

[30] Samek, Milo PhD, "Dynamic binding in C++," page 74 (this→*myState)(e).
[31] "Agile Programming: Design to Accommodate" – *IEEE Software* May/June 2005 – Dave Thomas.

know about the new feature. If the parent object is a COSA object, then the parent's rules can be changed to allow for the new feature.

In this example the COSA Extended BNF Table (Table 5.0), the columns called "True Actions" and "False Actions" are dynamically bound methods in this example. When the dynamic state is the same as the static state in line 8 of the engine, then the true behavior is dynamically bound[32] and executed at line 10. When control is returned to the engine, the trace at line 11 is called, followed by line 12, setting the temporal location for the next rule to be executed.

When the dynamic state is NOT the same as the static state in line 8 of the engine then the FALSE behavior is dynamically bound and executed at line 15. When control is returned to the engine, the FALSE trace at line 16 is called, followed by line 17, setting the temporal location for the next rule to be executed.

For example, if the first button clicked is a number then the dynamic state is not "fNeg44" and the engine will execute the false behavior "Ignore" at rule "rOper1" and transition to the next step using the entry in the Next False Rule column.

```
//                Static   True          Next True   False        Next False
//      Rules     State    Behavior        Rule      Behavior       Rule      Trace
  pBRT(rOpr1,    fNeg44,   Negate,      {0} rOpr1+1, Clr_Buf,    {1} rOpr1+1, 100);
  pBRT(rOpr1+1,  fDigit,   Any_Number,  {0} rOpr1+1, Ignore,     {1} rOpr1+3, 101);
  pBRT(rOpr1+2,  fDot59,   One_Period,  {0} rOpr1+3, Ignore,     {1} rOpr1+4, 102);
  pBRT(rOpr1+3,  fDigit,   Any_Number,  {0} rOpr1+3, Ignore,     {1} rOpr1+4, 103);
// clear
  pBRT(rOpr1+4,  fClEnt,   Clear_Entry, {0} rOpr1,   Ignore,     {1} rOpr1+5, 104);
  pBRT(rOpr1+5,  fClear,   Clear,       {0} rOpr1,   Push_Disp,  {1} rOpr8,   105);
// operations
  pBRT(rOpr8,    fAdd43,   Addition,    {0} rOpr2,   Ignore,     {1} rOpr8+1, 500);
  pBRT(rOpr8+1,  fSub44,   Subtraction, {0} rOpr2,   Ignore,     {1} rOpr8+2, 501);
  pBRT(rOpr8+2,  fMul42,   Multiply,    {0} rOpr2,   Ignore,     {1} rOpr8+3, 502);
  pBRT(rOpr8+3,  fDiv47,   Division,    {0} rOpr2,   Ignore,     {1} rErr,    503);
// next number
  pBRT(rOpr2,    fNeg44,   Negate,      {0} rOpr2+1, Clr_Buf,    {1} rOpr2+1, 700);
  pBRT(rOpr2+1,  fDigit,   Any_Number,  {0} rOpr2+1, Ignore,     {1} rOpr2+3, 701);
  pBRT(rOpr2+2,  fDot59,   One_Period,  {0} rOpr2+3, Ignore,     {1} rOpr2+4, 702);
  pBRT(rOpr2+3,  fDigit,   Any_Number,  {0} rOpr2+3, Ignore,     {1} rOpr2+4, 703);
// clear
  pBRT(rOpr2+4,  fClEnt,   Clear_Entry, {0} rOpr2,   Ignore,     {1} rOpr2+5, 704);
  pBRT(rOpr2+5,  fClear,   Clear,       {0} rOpr1,   Save_Disp,  {1} rResu,   705);
// equals
  pBRT(rResu,    fPer37,   Percent,     {0} rOpr1,   Ignore,     {1} rResu+1, 900);
  pBRT(rResu+1,  fEqual,   Equals,      {0} rOpr1,   Ignore,     {1} rResu+3, 901);
  pBRT(rResu+3,  fOper8,   Operate,     {1} rOpr8,   Ignore,     {0} rErr,    902);

  pBRT(rErr,     fErr86,   Error,       {0} rOpr1,   Error,      {0} rOpr1,   999);
end;
```

Table 5.0

COSA Extended BNF Rules

[32] Toward Open-World Software: Issues and Challenges – IEEE Computer Society – October 2006 – Luciano Baresi, Elisabetta Di Nitto, and Carlo Ghezzi.

5.3 The COSA Engine Implementation in C++

The segment of code below is the calculator engine implemented in Microsoft C++. The essence of the structure is nearly identical compared to the Borland/Delphi approach. The major difference is the pseudo object approach Microsoft uses in its implementation of the foundation class to access the calculator form objects. That is, Microsoft uses an IDC_EDIT1 value to look up the address of the calculator display object, "pEditWnd = GetDlgItem(IDC_EDIT1)," the result can be placed in the display object at line 17 below. Whereas, Borland/Delphi uses a true object path "formCalc.editdisplay.Text := sBuildNumber;" to place the result in the display object.

```
//************* C++ Implementation *******************

1   void aCalc::Run(int iState, LPCTSTR sDisplay) {
2     sNumber = sDisplay;
3     engCalc = 1;
4     dynamicState = iState;
5     while(engCalculate && engCalc){        //Local/Global preemption
6       if(Tbl[iTime].fState)
7       {
8               COSA_Trace(iTime);          // 33
9               (this->*(Tbl[iTime].True_Behavior))();
10              iTime = Tbl[iTime].Next_True;
11      } else {
12              COSA_Trace(-iTime);
13              (this->*(Tbl[iTime].False_Behavior))();
14              iTime = Tbl[iTime].Next_False;
15      }
16    }
17    pEditWnd->SetWindowText(_T(sBuildNumber)); // display
18  }
//************* C++ Implementation ***********************
```

Code Segment 5.1
C++ COSA Calculator Engine

---

[33] NOTE: There are times when the trace function call could be placed before the behaviors in the engine, as is the case in the C++ implementation.

5.4 The COSA Rules Table Implementation in C++

This implementation of the logic table in C++ is a little ugly. The ugliness is created by the fully qualified path to the action that is required by the language (Version 6.0 Developer Studio). Since Delphi does not require this extra work, I have not experimented with ways around this fully qualified requirement.

```
// Date= 12/4/2018
// Start of Generate Cpp Code File.
//                                        True           True        False       False;
//    Rule            State               T-Behavior     Next        Behavior       Next   Trace;
//-----------------------------------------------------------------------------------------------
  pGen( rOper1+  0,     &aCalc::fNegate,       &aCalc::pNegate,  rOper1+1,  &aCalc::pClrBuf, rOper1+1, 100);
  pGen( rOper1+  1,     &aCalc::fDigit,        &aCalc::pDigit,   rOper1+1,  &aCalc::pIgnore, rOper1+2, 110);
  pGen( rOper1+  2,     &aCalc::fDot,          &aCalc::pDot,     rOper1+3,  &aCalc::pIgnore, rOper1+4, 120);
  pGen( rOper1+  3,     &aCalc::fDigit,        &aCalc::pDigit,   rOper1+4,  &aCalc::pIgnore, rOper1+5, 130);
  pGen( rOper1+  4,     &aCalc::fClear,        &aCalc::pClear,   rOper1,    &aCalc::pIgnore, rOper1+5, 140);
  pGen( rOper1+  5,&aCalc::fClear_Entry,&aCalc::pClear_Entry,   rOper1,&aCalc::pPush_Disp,  rOper8,  150);
//-----------------------------------------------------------------------------------------------
  pGen( rOper8+  0,     &aCalc::fAdd,          &aCalc::pAdd,     rOper2,    &aCalc::pIgnore, rOper8+1, 900);
  pGen( rOper8+  1,     &aCalc::fSub,          &aCalc::pSub,     rOper2,    &aCalc::pIgnore, rOper8+2, 910);
  pGen( rOper8+  2,     &aCalc::fMul,          &aCalc::pMul,     rOper2,    &aCalc::pIgnore, rOper8+3, 920);
  pGen( rOper8+  3,     &aCalc::fDiv,          &aCalc::pDiv,     rOper2,    &aCalc::pIgnore, rOper2,   930);
//-----------------------------------------------------------------------------------------------
  pGen( rOper2+  0,     &aCalc::fNegate,       &aCalc::pNegate,  rOper2+1,  &aCalc::pClrBuf, rOper2+1, 700);
  pGen( rOper2+  ,      &aCalc::fDigit,        &aCalc::pDigit,   rOper2+1,  &aCalc::pIgnore, rOper2+2, 710);
  pGen( rOper2+  2,     &aCalc::fDot,          &aCalc::pDot,     rOper2+3,  &aCalc::pIgnore, rOper2+4, 720);
  pGen( rOper2+  3,     &aCalc::fDigit,        &aCalc::pDigit,   rOper2+4,  &aCalc::pIgnore, rOper2+5, 740);
  pGen( rOper2+  4,     &aCalc::fClear,        &aCalc::pClear,   rOper1,    &aCalc::pIgnore, rOper2+5, 740);
  pGen( rOper2+  5,&aCalc::fClear_Entry,&aCalc::pClear_Entry,   rOper2,&aCalc::pSave_Disp,  rResult,  750);
//-----------------------------------------------------------------------------------------------
  pGen( rResult+ 0,     &aCalc::fPerc,         &aCalc::pPerc,    rResult+1, &aCalc::pIgnore, rResult+1, 900);
  pGen( rResult+ 1,     &aCalc::fEqual,        &aCalc::pEqual,   rOper1,    &aCalc::pIgnore, rResult+2, 910);
  pGen( rResult+ 2,     &aCalc::fChain,        &aCalc::pChain,   rOper8,    &aCalc::pIgnore, rOper1,    920);
```

Table 5.1
C++ COSA Extended BNF

The rules are initialized differently in a C++ implementation. There is a macro that defines the structure, and the rules are created statically. The macro allows the pre-compiler to properly create the structure. Notice the ending comma; it is critical to making the macro work correctly. Also, notice the comma at the end of each line in the C++ rules above and the last rule does not have a comma. Depending on the strength of the compiler, these can be difficult to find if they are omitted. (There are similar issues when it comes to implementing this in Java.)

$$\#define\ rules(r,s,t,nt,f,nf,t)\ r,s,t,nt,f,nt,t,$$

In a multi-engine implementation in COSA, each engine has a control-flow table that contains the rules and their associated steps. The table in the calculator example uses seven columns. The seven columns are an indication of the structure of the engine. One column is used for the rule, and one column is used for the state. Two are used for true/false behaviors and two others are used for true/false transitions. The seventh and last column contains the trace value; in a large application this trace value could be something as large as a GUID[34].

In this particular implementation of the engine, the trace function is *"before"* the *"behaviors"* at lines 8 and 12. The rule is recorded in the object's trace mechanism before the step's operation has been performed.

5.5 Adding the Subordinate Percent Engine

The "Percent" operation only allows a sales tax type of calculation, i.e. value plus tax.

$$\$1.08 = \$1.00 \text{ plus } \$1.00 * (8\%)$$

In the ITE version of the calculator, the operations add, subtract, multiply, and divide are all allowed with percent. It is easy to add logic to an object by including a subordinate engine with rules and methods. In the initial design the "rResult" rule calls the proper operation through the dynamic bind variable. To perform the same functional flexibility, a subordinate engine and logical BNF are added to the original logic.

Every aspect of COSA can be viewed in a tree format. Because the percent procedures are relatively simple an interesting a new structure is introduced to the COSA Extended BNF Tree to define the actions of the data-flow procedures. Every section in COSA is labeled to keep them separate. Behind the scenes these structures are defined in XML and carry the necessary information to be complete.

{Control-Flow}	
Engine	= CalculatorPerc;
rPerc	= number * (iP_Add | iP_Sub | iP_Mul | iPDiv);
iP_Add	= pPerc_Add;
iP_Sub	= pPerc_Sub;

---

[34] http://en.wikipedia.org/wiki/Globally_Unique_Identifier

iP_Mul	= pPerc_Mul;
iP_Div	= pPerc_Mul;
{End Control-Flow}	
{Data-Flow}	
pPerc_Add	= (1 + number/100); engPerc_Off;
pPerc_Sub	= (1 - number/100); engPerc_Off;
pPerc_Mul	= number/100;engPerc_Off;
pPerc_Div	= pPerc_Mul;engPerc_Off;
{End Data-Flow}	

Tree 5.0
COSA Percent Engine

When the percent button is clicked it calls on the new subordinate engine's logic to determine what operation was entered prior to the percent key being entered. The BNF remains consistent with the application.

```
Procedure TCOSAcalc.Percent();
begin
  while (engPerc) AND (engGlobal) do
  begin
        if pOperArg00 = rPercent[iTime].pOperState then
        Begin
                rPercent[iTime].pTrueRule;        // Dynamically True Behavior
                True_Trace(iTime);                // TRUE TRACE SOLID
                iTime := rPercent[iTime].iTrueRule;  // Next True Rule Time
        end else
        Begin
                rPercent[iTime].pFalseRule;       // Dynamically False Behavior
                False_Trace(iTime);               // FALSE TRACE DASHED
                iTime := rPercent[iTime].iFalseRule; // Next False Rule Time
        end;
  sBuildNumber := FloatToStr(fNumber);
  bEngine := FALSE;                               // Turn Main Engine Off
end;
```

Code Segment 5.2
Delphi COSA Percent Engine

The logic in the percent engine is simple. If the operation is percent-addition, then the dynamic token created will match the static state "iP_Add". The calculation is completed in the procedure "pPerc_Add" shown below which also turns off the percent engine. The two other percent calculations perform their same respective actions. The next false action on each rule is to skip-chain through the logic looking for a dynamic-static state match.

If a match is not found, then the final false action is to call the error routine.

Rule	Static State	True Action	Next True Rule	False Action	Next False Rule	Trace
rPerc,	iP_Add,	pPerc_Add,	rPerc+1,	Ignore,	rPerc+1,	1100
rPerc+1,	iP_Sub,	pPerc_Sub,	rPerc+1,	Ignore,	rPerc+2,	1101
rPerc+2,	iP_Mul,	pPerc_Mul,	rPerc+3,	Ignore,	rPerc+3,	1102
rPerc+3,	iP_Div,	pPerc_Mul,	rPerc+3,	Error,	rPerc+3,	1103

Table 5.2
Percent Extended BNF Rules

Listed here are the new procedures that are required to support a more robust percent type calculation:

```
Procedure TCOSAcalc.pPerc_Add();        // 1100
Begin
  fNumber := fNumber * (1.0 + fDisplay/100.0);
  engPerc := FALSE;
end;
procedure TCOSAcalc.pPerc_Sub();        // 1101
Begin
  fNumber := fNumber * (1.0 – fDisplay/100.0);
  engPerc := FALSE;
end;
procedure TCOSAcalc.pPerc_Mul();        // 1102
begin
  fNumber := fNumber * fDisplay/100.0;
```

```
    engPerc := FALSE;
  end;
```

Code Segment 5.3
Percent Calculation

5.6 The Final BNF Definition

There are two engines that run in the application now, the principle calculator engine, and whenever a percent operation is requested, the percent engine is engaged.

Engines	= CalculatePercent;
Engine	= Calc;
:Calc	= rOper1 rOper8 rOper2 rResult?;
rOper1 (100)	= fNeg44?::ClrBuf fDigit*(fDot59 fDigit+)?
	(fClEnt? | fClear?::pPush) ;
fDigit	= (0|1|2|3|4|5|6|7|8|9)*;
rOper8 (500)	= fAdd43 | fSub44 | fMul42 | fDiv47;
rOper2 (700)	= fNeg44?::ClrBuf fDigit*(fDot59 fDigit+)?
	(fClEnt? | fClear?::pSave) ;
rResult (900)	= (fPerc37 | fEqual | fChain);
fChain	= rOper8
fClrEnt	= Clear the current display and value
fClear	= fClrEnt & restart
pPush	= Save the current displayed value
pSave	= Save the last calculation result
Engine	= Percent;
Percent	= rPerc;
rPerc (1100)	= number * (iP_Add | iP_Sub |
	iP_Mul | iPDiv);

Tree 5.1

Final COSA Extended BNF

The final Tree 5.1 does not show the control-flow sections like "[4,5]" so the focus is kept on the BNF structure of the logic.

5.7 Summary

The COSA engine implementation is consistent across languages. The COSA engine is truly a software component that can be used ubiquitously across the spectrum of applications. It can also be implemented as a subordinate engine expanding the logic of an object or procedural implementation. The flexibility offered by the COSA engine also includes the ability to dynamically turn the engine's trace on and off by replacing the trace procedure call with dynamic binding to a trace method or an "ignore" method.

Chapter 6
The COSA Methods in Detail

Chapter 6 covers what is left of traditional code development when the COSA engine and table have been implemented in a modeling tool. The part that remains to be manually coded is manipulation of the data. In domain-specific examples this can be as simple as drag and drop within a modeling tool. In an accounting application, this is the formula. In an engineering application, this is the equation. Each procedure or function is synchronized with a class definition and the control-flow defined by the COSA extended BNF.

6.1 The Methods in the GUI Class

There are two sections in the data-flow of this application: the GUI and the Logic. The GUI interfaces through the TformCalc Class. This class contains the "on-click" methods that are controlled by the Windows Message Loop as the buttons' event handlers. These "on-click" event handlers, like the multiply button event, are the access points to the COSA engine as shown in the following code segments. The "OnActivate" action is used to create the logic associated with the calculator form. This dynamic creation of the rules shown here is different from the C++ static approach.

```
Procedure TformCalc.CreateCOSA_OnActivate(Sender: Tobject);
begin
  objCOSA := TCOSAcalc.Create;
  objCOSA.CreateRules();      // create rules at runtime
end;
```

The Delphi GUI development environment creates the following procedures when the "on-click" event property is chosen. Each name is then edited to relate to the various buttons. The numbers have a single "on-click" event that provides access to the text captions the buttons display. This one button handler then passes the text to the parser token for the BNF logic tree. The "Sender: Tobject" provides access to the button text through the Caption[1] property. That text is a number in ASCII form.

```
procedure TformCalc.GetNumber_OnClick(Sender: Tobject);
var
  Argument : string;
begin
  Argument := TButton(Sender).Caption[1];  // get number from button
  objCOSA.Run(1,'0');
end;
```

The following "on-click" events are for the non-numbers. A numeric code was used for token values and the ASCII value where possible, like 43 decimal for the plus sign, to indicate the token's actual value when comparing the expected state to the dynamic state.

```
procedure TformCalc.SelectClear_OnClick(Sender: Tobject);
begin
  objCOSA.Run(11,'');
end;
```

```
procedure TformCalc.SelectClearEntry_OnClick(Sender: Tobject);
begin
  objCOSA.Run(12,'');
end;
```

```
procedure TformCalc.SelectAddition_OnClick(Sender: Tobject);
begin
 objCOSA.run(43,'');
end;
procedure TformCalc.SelectSubtraction_OnClick(Sender: Tobject);
```

```
begin
  objCOSA.run(44,'');
end;


procedure TformCalc.SelectMultiply_OnClick(Sender: Tobject);
begin
  objCOSA.run(42,'');
end;


procedure TformCalc.SelectDivide_OnClick(Sender: Tobject);
begin
  objCOSA.run(47,'');
end;


procedure TformCalc.SelectEquals_OnClick(Sender: Tobject);
begin
  objCOSA.run(13,'');
end;


procedure TformCalc.SelectPercent_OnClick(Sender: Tobject);
begin
  objCOSA.run(37,'');
end;
```

For the period "on-click" event the ASCII character gets passed to the engine and is used to build the number string. When the number string gets converted to a floating-point number the period is an essential part of the conversion.

```
Procedure TformCalc.SelectPeriod_OnClick(Sender: Tobject);
begin
  objCOSA.run(59,'.');
end;
```

The following method is simply used to clean up and release memory space after the application is done and shutting down.

```
Procedure TformCalc.CloseTraceFile_OnClose(Sender: Tobject;
var Action: TcloseAction);
begin
  closefile(TRACE_FILE);
  objCOSA.Destroy;
end;
```

6.2 The Methods in the Logic Class

The COSA object "objCOSA" is created by a call from the TFormCalc class to the TCOSAcalc class constructor. The logic for the Calculator is created dynamically using the object "objCOSA" to call the "CreateRules" procedure.

```
Procedure TformCalc.CreateCOSA_OnActivate(Sender: Tobject);
begin
  objCOSA := TCOSAcalc.Create;
  objCOSA.CreateRules();
end;
```

The procedure "pMCM" dynamically fills the logic array "rRule" with the defined COSA rules. The "pMCM" procedure defines the structure of the COSA Extended BNF Table to correspond to the structure of the COSA engine.

```
procedure TCOSAcalc.pMCM(iTime : integer; fState : fFunctionType;
    pTrueRule : pProcedureType; iTrueRule : integer;
    pFalseRule : pProcedureType; iFalseRule : integer;
    iTrace : integer);
begin
```

```
rRule[iTime] := TCOSARules.Create;
rRule[iTime].iTime := iTime;
rRule[iTime].fState := fState;
rRule[iTime].pTrueRule := pTrueRule;
rRule[iTime].iTrueRule := iTrueRule;
rRule[iTime].pFalseRule := pFalseRule;
rRule[iTime].iFalseRule := iFalseRule;
rRule[iTime].iTrace := iTrace;
end;
```

The procedure "CreateRules" uses the "pMCM" procedure to dynamically create the COSA rules making the rules ready for runtime logic execution.

//	Static	True		Next True	False		Next False	
// Rules	State	Behavior		Rule	Behavior		Rule	Trace
pBRT(rOpr1,	fNeg44,	Negate,	{0}	rOpr1+1,	Clr_Buf,	{1}	rOpr1+1,	100);
pBRT(rOpr1+1,	fDigit,	Any_Number,	{0}	rOpr1+1,	Ignore,	{1}	rOpr1+2,	101);
pBRT(rOpr1+2,	fDot59,	One_Period,	{0}	rOpr1+3,	Ignore,	{1}	rOpr1+4,	102);
pBRT(rOpr1+3,	fDigit,	Any_Number,	{0}	rOpr1+3,	Ignore,	{1}	rOpr1+4,	103);
// clear								
pBRT(rOpr1+4,	fClEnt,	Clear_Entry,	{0}	rOpr1,	Ignore,	{1}	rOpr1+5,	104);
pBRT(rOpr1+5,	fClear,	Clear,	{0}	rOpr1,	Push_Disp,	{1}	rOpr8,	105);
// operations								
pBRT(rOpr8,	fAdd43,	Addition,	{0}	rOpr2,	Ignore,	{1}	rOpr8+1,	500);
pBRT(rOpr8+1,	fSub44,	Subtraction,	{0}	rOpr2,	Ignore,	{1}	rOpr8+2,	501);
pBRT(rOpr8+2,	fMul42,	Multiply,	{0}	rOpr2,	Ignore,	{1}	rOpr8+3,	502);
pBRT(rOpr8+3,	fDiv47,	Division,	{0}	rOpr2,	Ignore,	{1}	rErr,	503);
// next number								
pBRT(rOpr2,	fNeg44,	Negate,	{0}	rOpr2+1,	Clr_Buf,	{1}	rOpr2+1,	700);
pBRT(rOpr2+1,	fDigit,	Any_Number,	{0}	rOpr2+1,	Ignore,	{1}	rOpr2+2,	701);
pBRT(rOpr2+2,	fDot59,	One_Period,	{0}	rOpr2+3,	Ignore,	{1}	rOpr2+4,	702);
pBRT(rOpr2+3,	fDigit,	Any_Number,	{0}	rOpr2+3,	Ignore,	{1}	rOpr2+4,	703);
// clear								
pBRT(rOpr2+4,	fClEnt,	Clear_Entry,	{0}	rOpr2,	Ignore,	{1}	rOpr2+5,	704);
pBRT(rOpr2+5,	fClear,	Clear,	{0}	rOpr1,	Save_Disp,	{1}	rResu,	705);
// equals								
pBRT(rResu,	fPer37,	Percent,	{0}	rOpr1,	Ignore,	{1}	rResu+1,	900);
pBRT(rResu+1,	fEqual,	Equals,	{0}	rOpr1,	Ignore,	{1}	rResu+2,	901);
pBRT(rResu+2,	fOper8,	Operate,	{1}	rOpr8,	Ignore,	{0}	rErr,	902);
pBRT(rErr,	fErr86,	Error,	{0}	rOpr1,	Error,	{0}	rOpr1,	993);

Table 6.0

The following methods are dynamically bound by the engine and are contained in the logic class "TCOSAcalc." The private methods in the data-flow are simple, using no parameters for this particular application. Each method does one thing for the state and does it well.

The "negate" method puts the "-" at the beginning of ASCII number about to be built and turns the engine off. When the engine is turned off, the display is updated using the following statement:

formCalc.editdisplay.Text := sBuildNumber;

The following procedures "Negate", "Any_Number", and "One_Period" are the three routines that build the first and second operand as strings. Notice the corresponding trace number is associated with each procedure.

```
procedure TCOSAcalc.Negate();                    // 100
Begin
  sBuildNumber := '-';
  bEngine := FALSE;
end;


procedure TCOSAcalc.Any_Number();              // 101
Begin
  sBuildNumber := sBuildNumber + sArgValue;
  bEngine := FALSE;
end;



procedure TCOSAcalc.One_Period();              // 102
Begin
  sBuildNumber := sBuildNumber + sArgValue;
  bEngine := FALSE;
end;
```

The "Any_Number" method concatenates the argument digit with the number being built, and then turns the engine off. The "One_Period" method concatenates a period to the number being built and turns the engine off. The next temporal step is the "Any_Number" at "rOper1+1". The "Any_Number" method is the same as the "rOper1+3", "rOper2+2", and "rOper2+4" steps. Likewise, the "Negate" method at step "rOper2+1" is the same as the "rOper1" step. That is, the first operand rule and the second operand rule use the same code to negate the displayed number.

The following four operations are pseudo operations. At the time they are executed their only role is to set up the proper operation (ADD, SUB, MUL, and DIVN) through the virtual pointer "pOperArg00", which will be dynamically bound and executed when the result rule is traversed. The methods of the "rOper8" rule like "Addition" are contained in trace numbers starting with 500. These are the four valid dynamic operator states allowed in our calculator example:

```
Procedure TCOSAcalc.Addition();                    // 500
Begin
  pOperArg00 := ADD;        //place addr addition in dynamic bind
end;


Procedure TCOSAcalc.Subtraction();                 // 501
Begin
  pOperArg00 := SUB; //place addr subtract in dynamic bind
end;


Procedure TCOSAcalc.Multiply();                    // 502
Begin
  pOperArg00 := MUL;        //place addr multiply in dynamic bind
end;


Procedure TCOSAcalc.Division();                    // 503
begin
  pOperArg00 := DIVN;       //place addr divide in dynamic bind
end;
```

The second operand methods are the same as the first operand, except the "Push_Disp" method replaces the "Save_Disp" method. The methods of the "Result" rule, "Percent", "Operate", and "Equal", are orthogonal operations on the two entered values.

The "Percent" procedure sets up the "PERC" procedure for a dynamic call within the try/except. The percent operation is executed when the percent button is clicked. If the operation does not fail, the "sBuildNumber" is loaded with the result. If the operation does fail, then the exception is displayed.

```
procedure TCOSAcalc.Percent();                    // 900
begin
pOperArg00 := PERC;// setup dynamic bind
try
  pOperArg00();                    // dynamic call
    sbuildNumber := FloatToStr(fNumber);
except
sbuildNumber:= 'Not A Number.';
  dynamicState := 86;  // not Maxwell Smart
  end;
englLocal := FALSE;
end;
```

The mathematics in the percent statement is a little different from the other four operators. The "Percent" operation takes the result number and multiplies it by the entered percent divided by 100. Notice the trace number is subordinated to an indented column indicating its relationship to the primary percent procedure in the logic table.

```
Procedure TCOSAcalc.PERC();                // 900
Begin
  fNumber := fNumber * (1.0 + fDisplay/100.0);
end;
```

The "Equals" method calls the dynamically bound generic method that is performing the correct operation between the first operand and the second operand and places the result in the display.

```
procedure TCOSAcalc.Equals();          // 901
begin
 formCalc.sNumber := '';
 try
 pOperArg00();        // call dynamically bound operation
   sbuildNumber := FloatToStr(fNumber);
  fNumber := 0.0;
except
  sbuildNumber:= 'Divide by Zero.';
  dynamicState := 86;   // not Maxwell Smart
  end;
 engLocal := FALSE;
 end;
```

The "Operate" method at trace 902 must find an operation rather than a percent or equal to allow it to continue operating on the result as in "8 + 5 * 9 / 2 + 23 - 1.4 =". Until the equal sign button is clicked, the operation can continue to chain.

```
procedure TCOSAcalc.Operate();              // 902
 begin
  sBuildNumber := '0';
 try
  pOperArg00();                   // bind to last operator
   sbuildNumber := FloatToStr(fNumber);
 except
 sbuildNumber:= 'Not A Number.';
   dynamicState := 86;  // not Maxwell Smart
  end;
 end;
```

Operand 1 builds the string variable "sNumber". When an operation is entered, the string contained in "sNumber" is converted to a floating-point number contained in "fNumber". Then operand 2 builds in the string "sNumber" until a result is selected, causing "sNumber" to be converted to "fDisplay". The math looks like this:

fNumber = fNumber **operation** fDisplay

"fNumber" is then put into the "sDisplay" and displayed in the calculator as the result. In a chain operation, the "sNumber" and "fDisplay" continue to be used until an equal operation is entered.

The following four functions are executed through the dynamic binding call "pOperArg00( )" when the equal button is clicked. The traditional ITE uses a similar approach in C++ that looks like "**(this➔*method())**" in its "Dispatch()" function.

```
procedure TCOSAcalc.ADD();          // 500
begin
  fNumber := fNumber + fDisplay;
end;


procedure TCOSAcalc.SUB();          // 501
begin
  fNumber := fNumber – fDisplay;
end;


Procedure TCOSAcalc.MUL();          // 502
begin
  fNumber := fNumber * fDisplay;
end;


procedure TCOSAcalc.DIVN();          // 503
begin
  fNumber := fNumber / fDisplay;
end;
```

The "Push_Disp" at trace 105F is called after the first operand has been entered and Clear Entry is not chosen. The calculator application manages the numbers as they are built behind the scenes. The try/except handles issues of "Not a Number," which can happen when operations are entered with no number or other operator maladies.

```
Procedure TCOSAcalc.Push_Disp();                    // 105
begin
  try
  fNumber := StrToFloat(sBuildNumber);
  sBuildNumber := '';
  except
  dynamicState := 86;  // Max again
  bEngine := FALSE;
  sBuildNumber := 'Not a Number.';
  end;
end;
```

The "Save_Disp" at trace 706 is called after the second operand has been entered and Clear Entry is not chosen in anticipation of a call to "Percent", "Equals", or "Operate". At this point in time the first operand is held in the variable "fNumber" and the second operand is held in the variable "fDisplay". The first and second operand rules use the same procedures up to the point where the entered strings are converted to floating point numbers.

```
procedure TCOSAcalc.Save_Disp();                    // 705
begin
  try
  fDisplay := StrToFloat(sBuildNumber);
  sBuildNumber := '0';
  except
  dynamicState := 86;  // and yet again
  bEngine := FALSE;
  sBuildNumber := 'Not a Number.';
  end;
end;
```

The administrative task of controlling the engine is by a simple Boolean state "bEngine" being turned on and off.

```
Procedure TCOSAcalc.Engine_Off();
begin
  bEngine := FALSE;
end;
```

The "CE" button only needs to clear the "sBuildNumber." The "sBuildNumber" is the operand being built.

```
Procedure TCOSAcalc.Clear_Entry();          // 104 & 705
begin
  sBuildNumber := '0';
  bEngine := FALSE;
end;
```

6.3 The Power of Temporal Logic

Setting the "fNumber" to floating point zero is not necessary because "fNumber" is overwritten as a part of the data manipulation in all the procedures that create the value "fNumber." All the procedures that use "fNumber" to accumulate cannot be reached after a "Clear_Entry" or "Clear" without going through one of the procedures that create the value and thereby overwrite the previous value. The following is a partial COSA Extended BNF Table showing the first operand logic for reference.

//
//Rule
//Step
// Operand 1
	Static
	State
		True
		Actions
			Next
			True
			Rule
				False
				Actions
					Next
					False
					Rule
						Trace

rOper1,	fNeg44,	Negate,	rOper1+1,	Ignore,	rOper1+1,	100
rOper1+1,	fDigit,	Any_Number,	rOper1+1,	Ignore,	rOper1+2,	101
rOper1+2,	fDot59,	One_Period,	rOper1+3,	Ignore,	rOper1+4,	102
rOper1+3,	fDigit,	Any_Number,	rOper1+3,	Ignore,	rOper1+4,	103
rOper1+4,	fClEnt,	Clear_Entry,	**rOper1,**	Ignore,	rOper1+5,	104
rOper1+5,	fClear,	Clear,	**rOper1,**	Push_Disp,	rOper8,	105

Table 6.1
First Operand Logic

The real difference between "Clear_Entry" and "Clear" is in the execution of the temporal logic. When the button CE is clicked the temporal logic in "rOper1" returns "iTime" to the operand rule at "rOper1". The temporal logic at the use of "Clear" returns "iTime" to the first operand rule "rOper1" . So, for the *first* operand rule, the procedures "Clear_Entry" and "Clear" could be the same.

```
Procedure TCOSAcalc.Clear();                    // 105 & 706
begin
  fNumber := 0.0;              // not necessary.
  sBuildNumber := '0';
  bEngine := FALSE;
end;
```

The second operand logic is repeated below. When the button CE is clicked the temporal logic in "rOper2" returns "iTime" to the operand rule at "rOper2". The temporal logic in "rOper2" at the use of "Clear" returns "iTime" to the first operand rule "rOper1" just like "Clear" in "rOper1". For the *second* operand rule the procedures "Clear_Entry" and "Clear" are *also* the same.

//Rule //Step	Static State	True Actions	Next True Rule	False Actions	Next False Rule	Trace
// Operand 2						
rOper2,	fNeg44,	Negate,	rOper2+2,	Ignore,	rOper2+2,	700
rOper2+1,	fDigit,	Any_Number,	rOper2+2,	Ignore,	rOper2+3,	701
rOper2+2,	fDot59,	One_Period,	rOper2+4,	Ignore,	rOper2+5,	702
rOper2+3,	fDigit,	Any_Number,	rOper2+4,	Ignore,	rOper2+5,	703
rOper2+4,	fClEnt,	Clear_Entry,	**rOper2+1,**	Ignore,	rOper2+6,	704
rOper2+5,	fClear,	Clear,	**rOper1,**	Save_Disp,	rOper2+7,	705

Table 6.2
Second Operand Logic

The logic is the only difference between the procedures "Clear_Entry" and "Clear". These two routines can be combined into one, reducing the size of the application. These discoveries are important to engineers working in real-time where cycles count; they are a lot easier to find when the logic is separate from the data manipulation.

6.4 The GUI Form Class

The Borland / Delphi developer environment makes this part of experimenting fairly easy. The variables beginning with "TformCalc" down to the "private" are all generated from the drag and drop process of creating the calculator form. The task of connecting the GUI to the logic is very simple, each "on-click" event calls the COSA Engine.

```
TformCalc = class(Tform)
  panelMain: Tpanel;
  tabPageControl: TpageControl;  tabCalculator: TtabSheet;
  editDisplay: Tedit;  tabTraceLogic: TtabSheet;  listStateDisplay: TlistBox;
  Button0: Tbutton;  Button1: Tbutton;  Button2: Tbutton;
  Button3: Tbutton;  Button4: Tbutton;  Button5: Tbutton;
  Button6: Tbutton;  Button7: Tbutton;  Button8: Tbutton;
  Button9: Tbutton;  ButtonC: Tbutton;  ButtonCE: Tbutton;
  ButtonSubtract: Tbutton;  ButtonDivide: Tbutton;  ButtonPercent: Tbutton;
  ButtonEquals: Tbutton;  ButtonMultiply: Tbutton;  ButtonAddition: Tbutton;
  ButtonPeriod: Tbutton;
```

```
procedure SelectZero_OnClick(Sender: Tobject);
procedure SelectOne_OnClick(Sender: Tobject);
procedure SelectTwo_OnClick(Sender: Tobject);
procedure SelectThree_OnClick(Sender: Tobject);
procedure SelectFour_OnClick(Sender: Tobject);
procedure SelectFive_OnClick(Sender: Tobject);
procedure SelectSix_OnClick(Sender: Tobject);
procedure SelectSeven_OnClick(Sender: Tobject);
procedure SelectEight_OnClick(Sender: Tobject);
procedure SelectNine_OnClick(Sender: Tobject);
procedure CreateCOSA_OnActivate(Sender: Tobject);
procedure SelectClear_OnClick(Sender: Tobject);
procedure SelectClearEntry_OnClick(Sender: Tobject);
procedure SelectAddition_OnClick(Sender: Tobject);
procedure SelectSubtraction_OnClick(Sender: Tobject);
procedure SelectMultiply_OnClick(Sender: Tobject);
procedure SelectEquals_OnClick(Sender: Tobject);
procedure SelectPercent_OnClick(Sender: Tobject);
procedure SelectPeriod_OnClick(Sender: Tobject);
procedure SelectDivide_OnClick(Sender: Tobject);
procedure CloseTraceFile_OnClose(Sender: Tobject; var Action: TcloseAction);
private
   { Private declarations }
   rCalc, rErr, rDone : integer;
   dynamicState, iTime : Integer;
   sNumber, sDisplay : String;
public
   { Public declarations }
   objCOSA : TCOSAcalc;
end;
```

TformCalc Class

6.5 The COSA Calculator Class

The TCOSAcalc is the work class with all the logic defined in the COSA Extended BNF Table (Extended BNF). Interface access is granted through the procedure "Run". The

64

"Run" procedure provides the "on-click" state and an ASCII character to the engine. A point of note is the "pOperArg00": "pProcedureType" definition. This is used to dynamically bind the proper operation when the equal sign is clicked.

Another point of note is the "rRule : Array of type TCOSArules". This array contains the rules defined by the Extended BNF.

rOper1, rOper8, rOper2, rResult, rError : integer;

The row addresses are defined by the rules in the Extended BNF. The first row "rOper1" is set to zero. Rule "rOper1" has seven physical states. The "rOper8" is defined as "rOper1" plus 7. The rule "rOper2" is defined as "rOper8" plus 4. Whenever a row is added to a rule, the base of the following rule must be updated. For example, if a square root rule is added to "rOper8", then the "rOper2" rule would have five steps. And rule "rOper2" would be defined as "rOper8" plus 5.

```
procedure TCOSAcalc.CreateRules();
begin
{$INCLUDE 'Create_Data.inc'}
        rOper1 := 0;                     // First Operand Rule
        rOper8 := rOper1 + 7;            // Operation Rules
        rOper2 := rOper8 + 4;            // Second Operand Rule
        rResult := rOper2 + 8;           // Result Rules
        rError  := rResult + 3;          // Error Handler Rules
o o o
COSA Extend BNF Rules table goes here…
//*********** COSA Framework for Rules to Run In **********
  TCOSAcalc = class(TCOSARules)     // inherits from
  public
 constructor Create;
 destructor Destroy; override;
  procedure Run(intState : integer; sNumber : String);
 private
        dynamicState, iIndex : integer;
        iAdd43, iSub44, iMul42, iDiv47, iPer37, iNeg44 : integer;        // Static States
        iDigit, iDot59, iClEnt, iPush, iSave, iChain, iOff : integer;    // Static States
```

```
        iClear, iErr86, iEqual, rOper1, rOper8, rOper2, rResult, rError : integer;
        bEngine : boolean;  fNumber, fDisplay, fTrace : real;
        pOperArg00 : pProcedureType;                        //    FOR    DYNAMIC
BINDING
        sReturnDisplay, sBuildNumber : String;
        strTrueBehavior : Array 0..22 of String;
        strFalseBehavior : Array 0..22 of String;
        rRule : Array 0..22 of TCOSARules;               // COSA Extended BNF RULES
        TRACE_FILE : TextFile;
private
   procedure pMCM(iTime : integer; iState : integer;
        pTrueRule : pProcedureType; iTrueRule : integer;
        pFalseRule : pProcedureType; iFalseRule : integer;
        iTrace : integer);
   procedure ADD();              // 500
   procedure SUB();              // 501
   procedure MUL();              // 502
   procedure DIVN();             // 503
   procedure PERC();             // 900
   procedure Negate();     // builds negative number              // 100
   procedure Any_Number();   // build integer and fraction        // 101
   procedure One_Period();   // adds decimal point                // 102
// procedure Any_Number(); // build integer and fraction          // 103
   procedure Clear_Entry();                                       // 104
   procedure Clear();                                             // 105
   procedure Push_Disp();                                         // 105
   procedure pAddition();                                         // 500
   procedure pSubtraction();                                      // 501
   procedure pMultiply();                                         // 502
   procedure pDivision();                                         // 503
// procedure pNegate();          // builds negative number        // 700
// procedure pAny_Number(); // build integer and fraction         // 701
// procedure pOne_Period(); // adds decimal point                 // 702
// procedure pAny_Number(); // build integer and fraction         // 703
// procedure pClear_Entry();                                      // 704
// procedure pClear();                                            // 705
```

```
procedure pSave_Disp();                                    // 705
procedure pPercent();                                      // 900
procedure pEquals();                                       // 901
procedure pOperate();                                      // 902
procedure pUnknown();                                      // 993
procedure pError();                                        // 902
procedure True_Trace(iTime : integer);
        procedure False_Trace(iTime : integer);
procedure CreateRules();
procedure pDone();
procedure pIgnore();
end;
```

6.6 The COSA Rules Class

The TCOSARules class defines the column structure for the Extended BNF Rules Table. The first line after the comment

"pProcedureType = **procedure** of Object;"

is the definition that allows the application to dynamically bind at runtime to the true and false behaviors. The "iTime" definition is a vestigial column as the comment says. In a table it is only used as a placeholder to show the step-row location. When the rules are created dynamically in the "CreateRules" method the rule base "rOper1" is set to zero.

```
// ********************* COSA Rules Definition *******************
  pProcedureType = procedure of Object;
  fButtonType = function : Tobject;
  TCOSARules = class
    public
    private
      iTime : integer;    // Temporal Component (vestigial place keeper)
      iState : integer;                   // Expected State Value
```

```
          pTrueRule : pProcedureType;        // True Behavior
          iTrueRule : integer;               // Next iTime on True
          pFalseRule : pProcedureType;       // False Behavior
          iFalseRule : integer;              // Next iTime on False
          iTrace : integer;                  // Trace Value or Code
   end;
```

The second column is the static state definition. The third column is the true behavior definition. The forth column is the definition for next true temporal transition. The fifth column is the false behavior definition. The sixth column defines the next false temporal transition. The last column is the trace type.

6.7 Summary

This chapter covers the procedures that manipulate the data. There are three complex procedures. First is the run procedure that contains the engine. Second is the procedure that creates the rules. The rules structure for the COSA Extended BNF Table is defined as a class. Each row of the COSA Extend BNF class is dynamically created and placed in an array in the pMCM procedure. The third complex procedure is the group of results procedures.

The framework provided by Borland makes access to the Windows operating system easy. Using Delphi's drag and drop approach it is very easy to create the user calculator interface. Creating the "on-click" events provides the interface to the logic. Borland, in their Delphi implementation, have a naming convention that I have tried to follow in this text. It is important to label every variable with a prefix-Polish notation. This approach allows code manufacture to use the same name, creating a relationship.

Chapter 7

COSA Trace

Once an application has begun testing the ability to trace the execution of the logic could be a paramount task. In the design of an application, testing should always be a consideration. Even if trace is designed into an application, enormous efforts can be required to get the right information about the runtime application. The spatial approach to application implementation, with the distributed "if-then-else" logic throughout the application, makes the task of a comprehensive trace almost impossible at design time or after the fact. The COSA trace has solved this very complex problem.

The COSA implementation includes an integral trace as a part of the architecture. With trace integral to the architecture, the trace of documentation and runtime considerations are handled to a greater level of detail than many standards require. With the separation of software components into engine, rules table, and procedures, the trace documentation can specify exactly where a change or problem occurred. For example, trace documentation can explain that the logic was changed to handle additional use cases. And, because the logic is separate from the data manipulation the new use cases may not require any changes to the supporting procedures.

Another feature of integral trace is the ability of a help-mechanism to understand the flow of logic that put a particular user in a specific part of the application's logic. This kind of tracking information can be valuable for understanding consumer logic, user logic, or hacker logic. Systems will become more secure when temporal logic is built into them.

The COSA Extended BNF Table is repeated here to help with the analysis of dynamic trace that follows.

Rule	Static State	True Behavior	Next True Rule	False Behavior	Next False Rule	Trace
// Operand 1						
rOper1,	fNeg44,	pNegate,	rOper1+1,	pIgnore,	rOper1+1,	100
rOper1+1,	fDigit,	pAny_Number	rOper1+1,	pIgnore,	rOper1+2,	101
rOper1+2,	fDot59,	pOne_Period	rOper1+3,	pIgnore,	rOper1+4,	102
rOper1+3,	fDigit,	pAny_Number	rOper1+3,	pIgnore,	rOper1+4,	103
rOper1+4,	fClEnt,	pClear_Entry	rOper1,	pIgnore,	rOper1+5,	104
rOper1+5,	fClear,	pClear,	rOper1,	pPush_Disp,	rOper8,	105
// Operation						
rOper8,	fAdd43,	pAddition,	rOper2,	pIgnore,	rOper8+1,	500
rOper8+1,	fSub44,	pSubtraction,	rOper2,	pIgnore,	rOper8+2,	501
rOper8+2,	fMul42,	pMultiply,	rOper2,	pIgnore,	rOper8+3,	502
rOper8+3,	fDiv47,	pDivision,	rOper2,	pIgnore,	rError,	503
// Operand2						
rOper2,	fNeg44,	pNegate,	rOper2+1,	pIgnore,	rOper2+1,	700
rOper2+1,	fDigit,	pAny_Number	rOper2+1,	pIgnore,	rOper2+2,	701
rOper2+2,	fDot59,	pOne_Period	rOper2+3,	pIgnore,	rOper2+4,	702
rOper2+3,	fDigit,	pAny_Number	rOper2+3,	pIgnore,	rOper2+4,	703
rOper2+4,	fClEnt,	pClear_Entry	rOper2,	pIgnore,	rOper2+5,	704
rOper2+5,	fClear,	pClear,	rOper1,	pSave_Disp,	rResult,	705
// Result						
rResult,	fPer37,	pPercent,	rOper1,	pIgnore,	rResult+1,	900
rResult+1,	fEqual,	pEquals,	rOper1,	pIgnore,	rResult+2,	901
rResult+2,	fChain,	pOperate,	rOper8,	pOperate,	rOper8,	902
rError,	fErr86,	pUnknown,	rOper1,	pError,	rOper1,	993

Table 7.0
COSA Extended BNF Rules Table

7.1 Toward Fully Automated Testing

A testing scenario can be forecast from the final BNF (Tree 5.1) using the trace numbers that have been assigned. When the tests are run through the application the testing scenario should match the trace file. The test analysis file will look like final BNF with the trace numbers replacing the elements: 100? 101* (102 103+)? … This test analysis file allows for all possible scenarios that have been designed into the application. This approach also allows for the automatic generation of the test file since the individual states are coherent. The test generator knows to generate a negate "100?" in one scenario, zero or more integer-portions "101*" in another scenario, and optional decimal portions "(102103+)?" in another scenario.

Using the COSA approach to testing the location of source bugs[35] can be found faster and with more precision as the next few pages reveal. The COSA engine provides a centralized trace for each object than can be turned on and off or changed (dynamically bound) to different trace objects as needed, and each centralized trace can be customized to provide any level of detail to help with testing and debugging. The testing tools can include the generation of process maps to help understand performance density where logic or data tuning might help performance.

The potential cost reduction from an improved testing infrastructure, according to the referenced NIST paper (section 8-6), is $22.249 billion in 2002 dollars. Any improvement in testing is important to the quality of software. That number is interesting because it is only about one-third of the $59.5 billion 2002 dollars the industry loses due to bugs. In 2017 that number went over $1.1 trillion dollars.

7.2 The Ultimate Dynamic Trace

COSA trace can be as simple or elaborate as the testing requires. In this example everything of interest in the calculator example has been added to the trace AT ONE SINGLE POINT. Entering "-3.14159" results in the engine generating the following temporal trace:

T/F	Rule+	Engine	Static	Dynamic	Behavior	Trace	Result
+T	0;	Off;	S= 44;	D= 44;	pNegate;	100	N= -
+T	1;	Off;	S= 1;	D= 1;	pAny_Number;	101	N= -3
-F	1;	**On;**	**S= 1;**	**D= 59;**	pIgnore;	101	N= -3
+T	2;	Off;	S= 59;	D= 59;	pOne_Period;	102	N= -3.
+T	3;	Off;	S= 1;	D= 1;	pAny_Number;	**103**	N= -3.1
+T	3;	Off;	S= 1;	D= 1;	pAny_Number;	**103**	N= -3.14
+T	3;	Off;	S= 1;	D= 1;	pAny_Number;	**103**	N= -3.141
+T	3;	Off;	S= 1;	D= 1;	pAny_Number;	**103**	N= -3.1415
+T	3;	Off;	S= 1;	D= 1;	pAny_Number;	**103**	N= -3.14159

Trace 7.0
Calculator Operand 1

The engine is turned off and control is returned to the OS message loop after every step where the Engine column shows "Off". The third line of Trace 7.0 starts with –F, indicating

<hr>

[35] Gregory Tassey, "The Economic Impacts of Inadequate Infrastructure for Software Testing", May 2002, National Institute of Standards and Technology, Section 4.1.3, Page 4.3

a false behavior, the Engine column shows the engine remained "On". The control-flow logic is looking for a static state "1", the number building step. But the dynamic state had a value of 59, which is a period. The engine remained on and time moved to the next true step at Trace 102, the period static state value of 59. Satisfied with a match between static and dynamic, the engine is turned off. The trace example shows that step "rOper1+3", in *Table 7.0* on the previous page, of the first rule is repeatedly executed, and the "Trace" column shows that trace 103 is repeated five times. If a number is entered, the fractional portion of the number is built. This would also apply to step "rOper +1" in *Table 7.0* when building the integer portion of the number.

The next part of the example for the engine is to perform a subtraction operation by clicking on the "-". This results in the "on-click" event handler catching the operation and returning to the "temporal" location left by the previous operation.

In the following Trace 7.1, the first five events in the first column are false. There is not a match at static values "S= 1", "S= 12", "S= 11," "S= 1", and "S= 43", and only their false behaviors were executed. In the logic table these steps correspond to ending the concatenation of numbers that were building the fractional part of the number and looking for the operation. The column labeled Dynamic contains the "D= 44," which is the ASCII code for "-" (subtraction).

The true next step follows the "Subtraction" operation directly to the "Engine_Off" temporal trace number 700 in Trace 7.1 to allow the engine to be turned off. Control is returned to the "on click" event handler and back to the Windows message loop for the next event to be trapped.

T/F	Rule+	Engine	Static	Dynamic	Behavior	Trace	Result
-F	3;	On;	S= 1;	D= 44;	pIgnore;	103	N= -3.14159
-F	4;	On;	S= 12;	D= 44;	pIgnore;	104	N= -3.14159
-F	5;	On;	S= 11;	D= 44;	pIgnore;	105	N= -3.14159
-F	6;	On;	S= 1;	D= 44;	pPush_Disp;	105	N= -3.14159
-F	7;	On;	S= 43;	D= 44;	pIgnore;	500	N= -3.14159
+T	8;	On;	S= 44;	D= 1;	pSubtract;	501	N= -3.14159
+T	11;	Off;	S= 1;	D= 1;	pEng_Off;	**700**	N= -3.14159

Trace 7.1

Calculator Operation

In the Trace 7.2, the number "-2.14159" is entered. The second operand rule "rOper2", from *Table 7.0*, performs the same as the first operand rule. The second operand is built and displayed just as the first operand was built and displayed. Trace goes from 701 to 704. At 704 the trace is repeated, building the fractional part of the number.

T/F	Rule+	Engine	Static	Dynamic	Behavior	Trace	Result
+T	12;	Off;	S= 44;	D= 44;	pNegate;	701;	N= -
+T	13;	Off;	S= 1;	D= 1;	pAny_Number;	702;	N= -2
-F	13;	On;	S= 1;	D= 59;	pIgnore;	702;	N= -2
+T	14;	Off;	S= 59;	D= 59;	pOne_Period;	703;	N= -2.
+T	15;	Off;	S= 1;	D= 1;	pAny_Number;	704;	N= -2.1
+T	15;	Off;	S= 1;	D= 1;	pAny_Number;	704;	N= -2.14
+T	15;	Off;	S= 1;	D= 1;	pAny_Number;	704;	N= -2.141
+T	15;	Off;	S= 1;	D= 1;	pAny_Number;	704;	N= -2.1415
+T	15;	Off;	S= 1;	D= 1;	pAny_Number;	704;	N= -2.14159

Trace 7.2
Calculator Operand 2

When the equal sign is clicked, the proper "on-click" event handler calls the engine again starting at "rOper2+4", in *Table 7.0*. Since the dynamic state is looking for a token of value "13," the engine transitions from trace 704 through to trace 901. In *Table 7.0* this is in rule "rResult" at step 1. The result is then displayed, and the next true rule is back to "rOper1," which is back at the beginning of the logic in *Table 7.0*.

T/F	Rule+	Engine	Static	Dynamic	Behavior	Trace	Result
-F	15;	On;	S= 1;	D= 13;	pIgnore;	**704**;	N= -2.14159
-F	16;	On;	S= 12;	D= 13;	pIgnore;	705;	N= -2.14159
-F	17;	On;	S= 37;	D= 13;	pIgnore;	900;	N= -2.14159
+T	18;	Off	S= 13;	D= 13;	pEquals;	**901**;	N= -1

Trace 7.3

73

Calculator Results

The column labeled Behavior was added to the calculator application trace to provide a string listing of the behavior in addition to the trace number. A word compared to a number, when it comes to debugging logic, can be very valuable. When it comes to understanding the logic for debugging, it is useful to display the behavior in the trace: "a picture is worth a thousand words".

7.3 Dynamic Trace in the Application

The next few pages show a series of screen shots of the calculator and dynamic trace in action as the calculation of subtracting a negative number from a negative number is performed.

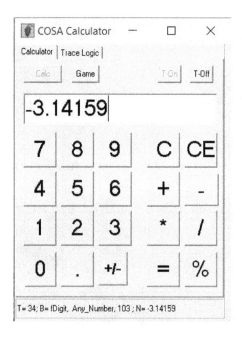

Figure 7.0

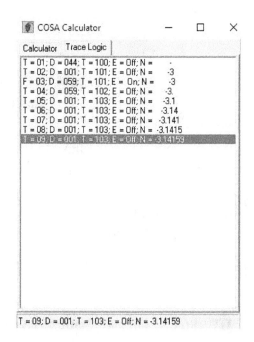

Figure 7.1

The negative number "-3.14159" is entered in Figure 7.0 creating the trace logic in Figure 7.1. The first column/value in Figure 7.1 is the True or False State displayed as a "T" or an "F." The second value is the temporal step displayed as "00", "01", "02", "03", etc., and the third value is the trace "T = 100" that is coded for each section going back to the specification: 100 for the first operand, 500 for the operator, 700 for the second operand, and 900 for the result rule. The fourth value is the string name of the behavior executed, and the last value in this particular implementation is the intermediate string value as it is built.

As the arithmetic operation continues, the last column displays the operand value built which includes the "-" subtraction operation when it is entered at "T= 12".

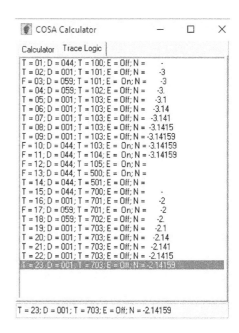

Figure 7.2   **Figure 7.3**

The number "-2.14519" has been entered in Figure 7.2. The operational trace in Figure 7.3 shows the actions of subtracting a negative number from the previous negative number.

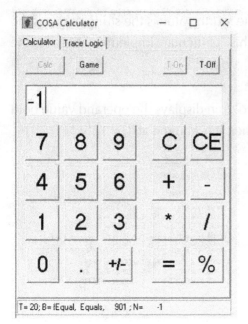

Figure 7.4

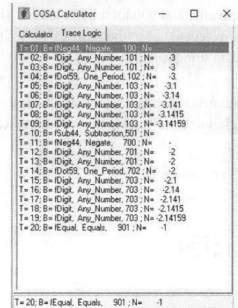

Figure 7.5

In a temporal approach implemented in a fully commercial GUI, the engineer can look at the UML class diagrams, the state diagrams, the BNF, the COSA logic-flow and data-flow, and be able to interact with trace in the animation of this entire process. Since the trace files can be very large it would be wise to provide full search capabilities to help in the debugging process.

7.4 Analyzing the Calculator Trace

When the "E=On" the engine is looking for a match. When the engine finds a match "E=Off" and control is returned to the Windows message loop. In the Trace 7.1 on the next page when E=Off the engine is "happy".

Notice the skip chain logic from temporal step "F= 04" to "F= 10" with "D= 044" (Subtraction). This sequence of logic is the engine looking for a match between the dynamic state and the static state. At F=03 the state is transitioning from having the number 3 entered to getting the decimal point D=059 and T=102. At T=04 trace T=103 there is a match a number has been entered and the engine turns off and the temporal pointer remains at T=103 indicating that the logic continues to expect a number. T=05 through T=09 the trace remains at T=103. At F=10 the subtract has been entered. The logic tests for digit F=10, clear F=11, clear entry F=12, F=13 addition, and F=14 where the subtraction is found.

Figure 7.4 shows the negative one (-1) result of subtracting a negative number from a negative number. The trace in Figure 7.5 of subtracting a negative number from a negative number is complete. As can be seen from this example, the trace can be extremely rich in its content. And since each engine has its own trace routines, it is easy to add or remove information relevant to the class or the object and its inheritance.

Figure 7.6 shows the code to produce the Elaborate Trace in the GUI trace and the file trace. The ability to create all the detail from a single point in the code has saved me hours of debugging.

```
procedure TCOSAcalc.True_Trace(iTime : integer);
var
  iIndex, iTrace : integer;
  sTraceString, strEngine : string;
begin
  iTrace := rRule[iTime].iTrace;
  sTraceString :=
          Format('T = %2.2d', [iCount]) +
          Format(': D = %3.3d', [iState]) +
          Format(': T = %3.3d', [iTrace]) +
          Format(': E = %3s', [strEngine]) +
          Format(': N = %8s', [sBuildNumber]);
  formCalc.tabPageControl.ActivePage.PageIndex := 1;
  formCalc.listStateDisplay.Items.Append(sTraceString);
  formCalc.StatusBar1.Panels.Items[0].Text := sTraceString;
  iIndex := formCalc.listStateDisplay.ItemIndex+1;
  formCalc.listStateDisplay.Selected[iIndex];
  formCalc.listStateDisplay.ItemIndex := iIndex;
  formCalc.tabPageControl.ActivePage.SetFocus;
  formCalc.tabPageControl.ActivePage.PageIndex := 0;
  WriteLn(TRACE_FILE, sTraceString);
end;
```

Figure 7.6 Elaborate Trace

Time					
True/False,	Dynamic,	Trace,	Engine	Result	
T = 01;	D = 044;	T = 100;	E = Off;	N =	-
T = 02;	D = 001;	T = 101;	E = Off;	N =	-3
F = 03;	D = 059;	T = 101;	E = On;	N =	-3
T = 04;	D = 059;	T = 102;	E = Off;	N =	-3.
T = 05;	D = 001;	T = 103;	E = Off;	N =	-3.1
T = 06;	D = 001;	T = 103;	E = Off;	N =	-3.14
T = 07;	D = 001;	T = 103;	E = Off;	N =	-3.141

T = 08;	D = 001;	T = 103;	E = Off;	N = -3.1415
T = 09;	D = 001;	T = 103;	E = Off;	N = -3.14159
F = 10;	D = 044;	T = 103;	E = On;	N = -3.14159
F = 11;	D = 044;	T = 104;	E = On;	N = -3.14159
F = 12;	D = 044;	T = 105;	E = On;	N =
F = 13;	D = 044;	T = 500;	E = On;	N =
T = 14;	D = 044;	T = 501;	E = Off;	N =
T = 15;	D = 044;	T = 700;	E = Off;	N = -
T = 16;	D = 001;	T = 701;	E = Off;	N = -2
F = 17;	D = 059;	T = 701;	E = On;	N = -2
T = 18;	D = 059;	T = 702;	E = Off;	N = -2.
T = 19;	D = 001;	T = 703;	E = Off;	N = -2.1
T = 20;	D = 001;	T = 703;	E = Off;	N = -2.14
T = 21;	D = 001;	T = 703;	E = Off;	N = -2.141
T = 22;	D = 001;	T = 703;	E = Off;	N = -2.1415
T = 23;	D = 001;	T = 703;	E = Off;	N = -2.14159
F = 24;	D = 013;	T = 703;	E = On;	N = -2.14159
F = 25;	D = 013;	T = 704;	E = On;	N = -2.14159
F = 26;	D = 013;	T = 705;	E = On;	N =
F = 27;	D = 013;	T = 900;	E = On;	N =
T = 28;	D = 013;	T = 901;	E = Off;	N = -1

Trace 7.1

7.5 The Ultimate Static Trace

To comply with various standards like Good Manufacturing Practice (GMP), ISO, DOD-Military and others, any changes made to software must be recorded. The COSA trace facility greatly enhances recording defects and tracking changes.   The trace element in each row of the COSA Extended BNF Rules Table provides a common point of reference. When any aspect of the application changes, the details are recorded at the logic level associated with each row. Recording defects and changes in an ITE application is difficult because a common point of reference is not available.

The Temporal Engineering trace mechanism can be turned on and off without the enormous side effects of the traditional Spatial Engineering approach.

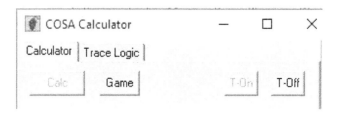

Figure 7.7

The "T-On" in dim mode indicates that trace is turned on the option "T-Off" and it can be used to dynamically turn off the trace.

The following code segment uses dynamic binding to control trace from the GUI. The lines containing "pTraceTrue" and "pTraceFalse" are the place holders for the calls to trace. The values "True_Trace", "False_Trace", and "Ignore" are the behaviors that can be executed from the engine. When "T-Off" is enabled the trace capability of the engine is disabled.

```
procedure TCOSAcalc.pTurnTraceOn();
begin
   pTraceTrue := True_Trace;
   pTraceFalse := False_Trace;
   Assign(TRACE_FILE, 'Calculator_Trace.txt');
   Rewrite(TRACE_FILE);
   WriteLn(TRACE_FILE, 'Date= ' + DateToStr(Date));
   WriteLn(TRACE_FILE, 'Start of Calc-Tic-Tac-Toe Trace File.');
   WriteLn(TRACE_FILE, 'True/False,  Dynamic,    Trace,     Result');
   WriteLn(TRACE_FILE);
end;
procedure TCOSAcalc.pTurnTraceOff();
begin
   pTraceTrue := Ignore1;
   pTraceFalse := Ignore1;
   try
      WriteLn(TRACE_FILE,'***** Turning Trace Off *****');
      CloseFile(TRACE_FILE);
   except
      ShowMessage('TRACE_FILE was not turned on.');
   end;
   iTraceState := 0;
end;
```

Figure 7.8 – Trace Dynamic Binding Code Segment

7.6 The Cost of Fixing Bugs

The following is from Synopsys.com: "Software Integrity"

> ... it was reported by the <u>Systems Sciences Institute at IBM</u>[36] that the cost to fix a bug found during implementation was around 6 times costlier than one identified during design. Furthermore, according to IBM, bugs found during the testing phase could be 15 times more costly than during design.

I agree with this 6 and 15 times more costly assessment. Because these numbers are based on the Spatial Engineering of software. When data manipulation is imbedded in the application every change or fix can have unintended consequences. The concept of coherent software has been around for years but the traditional approach to software development makes the coherent rule very difficult to adhere to with any consistency.

7.7 Summary

The COSA dynamic trace provides 100% coverage of the application's logic and can easily be turned on and off. The detail available to COSA static trace exceeds most recording standards for software changes. COSA trace can dramatically improve the quality of automated testing because the rules/steps provide proof of coverage in an architecture that reduces complexity to logic and the correctness of data manipulation as orthogonal components. Plus, the BNF and the trace number can be used to design the test suite. Each element in the trace references a behavior that is coherent which makes finding the bug that much easier.

The first seven chapters have introduced COSA as a powerful paradigm for specifying the rules of how to handle the dynamic behavior of reactive objects. Reactive objects are objects that respond to events, like the "on-click events", sent from other objects. The response of a COSA reactive object to an event depends on what rule and iTime the object is in when that the event occurred.

---

[36] https://www.researchgate.net/figure/255965523_fig1_Figure-3-IBM-System-Science-Institute-Relative-Cost-of-Fixing-Defects

Chapter 8

COSA vs. ITE –
Flow Analysis of Procedure Calls

The analysis of the procedure calls within these two vastly different implementations of the five-function calculator gives more insight to the differences between the spatial "If-Then-Else" approach to programming and the temporal COSA.

The COSA implementation of the calculator call analysis is shown in Figure 8.0. Notice that most of the calls are made directly from the run engine. The exception is where the operations are dynamically bound in the "Percent", "Equals", and "Operate" methods. An interesting observation is the COSA call diagram is very similar to the COSA state diagram. The similarity of the logic associated with the application comes from the dynamically bound COSA Extended BNF Rules Table. The call sequence really is the state diagram, but it lacks the temporal component. The state diagram shows each time a state is used, whereas, the call diagram only shows one use of a spatial state. Spatially, the "Any_Number" procedure is called from the runtime engine only once, even though temporally, the "Any_Number" routine is called four times as can be seen in the state diagram and COSA Extended BNF.

The temporal organization of this application is simple when compared to the complex spatial approach employed by traditional ITE software. A commercial tool[37] was used to extract the necessary information to create these call diagrams in Microsoft Visio. A call analysis was performed for both applications. The reports shown in Appendix A and B can be used to verify the call structure and relationships.

---

[37] CDOC Documentation Tool for C, C++ and Java, www.swbs.com and www.softwareblacksmiths.com using a feature called CCALL ™ caller/called hierarchy ("flow structure") between functions.

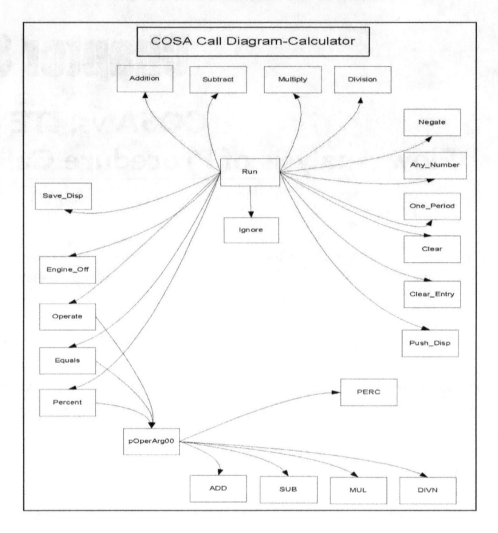

Figure 8.0
COSA Calculator Call Diagram

Figure 8.0 shows the temporal call diagram. Each of the routines may be called multiple times from the engine at the appropriate point in time based on the COSA logic table. The procedure "Negate" is used by both rules for the first and second operand. The only procedures that are unique between the first and second operand rules is the "Save_Disp" and the "Push_Disp" routines.

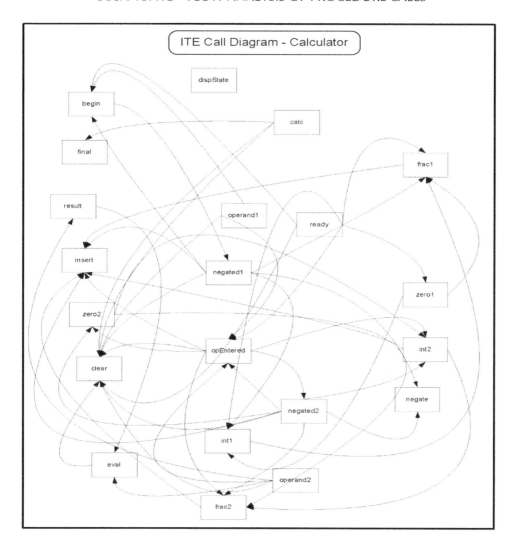

Figure 8.1

ITE Calculator Call Diagram

Graphically, Figure 8.1 represents a spatial call diagram of the ITE calculator. The complexity of this diagram comes from the need of the event to determine its state in the application. For example, the procedure "begin" is called from "ready" and "operand1." In the process of building the number "frac1"is called by "negated1," "ready," and "zero1." The procedure "insert" on the left of the diagram is called six times from six different procedures. The procedure "calc" doesn't show a call arrow but it is called from inside "begin" using a macro. The generalized ITE coding technique is difficult to understand, generate, secure, maintain, or improve without causing side effects and bugs.

Trace has been added to the temporal COSA in Figure 8.2. It is the two dashed lines running from the Run engine to the trace boxes. Trace coverage is 100% of all procedures called.

8.1 Testing the ITE Approach

According to a NIST report[38] the software industry spent one-third of its revenue fixing its products. Even so Bill Gates[39] once bragged; if cars were produced like software they would cost less and get much better gas mileage. While that may be true on the surface it does not speak to the quality of software. The NIST report points out that 302,450 Full Time Equivalent software engineers and computer programmers were engaged in fixing bugs every year. Considering that Figure 8.1 represents the standard for the software referenced in the NIST report one can see why so much time is spent debugging. But NIST refers to an inadequate infrastructure for software testing when in fact the industry has built a massive infrastructure around an ITE basis, which, realistically cannot be tested adequately. The report goes on to point out that up to $22 billion could be saved from infrastructure testing improvements.

---

[38] Gregory Tassey, "The Economic Impacts of Inadequate Infrastructure for Software Testing", May 2002, National Institute of Standards and Technology. Chapter 8, "National Impact Estimates"
[39] An urban legend starts http://www.snopes.com/humor/jokes/autos.asp about GM response.

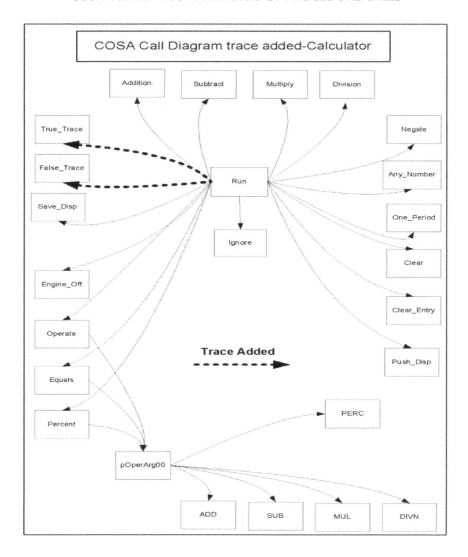

Figure 8.2
COSA Calculator Call Diagram with Trace Added

Both applications have been implemented using an object approach. Both applications provide the same functionality, but clearly there is a difference. The logic in COSA is temporal and produces organized diagrams. The logic in the traditional ITE spatial approach appears unorganized in this application. Trace in Figure 8.3 has been added to the ITE approach, but it still does not provide full coverage with several procedures ("eval", "clear", "zero2", and "negate") not called because it would make the diagram unreadable.

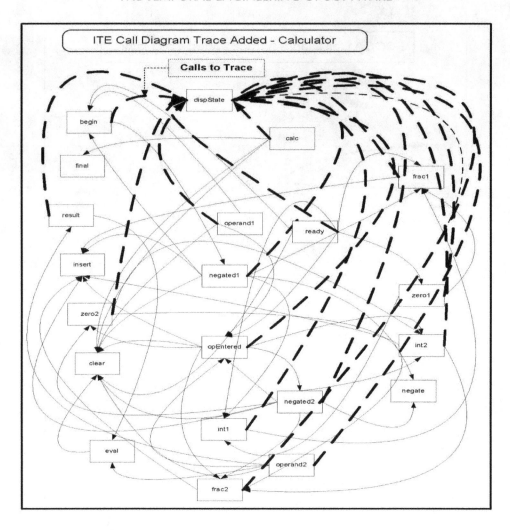

Figure 8.3
ITE Calculator Call Diagram with Trace Added

The complexity in Figure 8.3 is not artificial. There is no way to reduce the complexity of diagram by moving the procedures around because the definitions are spatial. The complexity is inherent in the ITE approach. Assuming that these two approaches (temporal and spatial) remain true to their inherent nature, one can see how billions of dollars[40] can be spent on software bugs using the ITE approach. Clearly, bad logic can create problems and complexity for any approach, but COSA provides an approach that is grounded in binary and temporal logic. Even good logic is difficult to understand

---

[40] http://www.nist.gov/public_affairs/releases/n02-10.htm; U.S. Department of Commerce's National Institute of Standards and Technology (NIST), the bugs and glitches cost the U.S. economy about $59.5 billion a year. – June 28, 2002

using the ITE approach. In an ITE application complexity cannot be reduced because the engineer cannot do one simple piece of logic. With ITE, adding any other functionality to a procedure increases the complexity of that procedure. With COSA, added functionality can be achieved through changing the Extended BNF Table logic without changing any procedure.

8.2 An Efficiency Comparison with ITE

With ITE the application does not have an inherent temporal component. Any ITE application must repeatedly test to determine where in the state sequence the execution is working. Referring to the ITE state diagram of Figure 4.3 the "negated1" (3) state is entered six times. This can be seen in the ITE Trace[41] Table 8.0 below between sequence 13 and 27. The "int1" (6) state is entered six times in the trace sequence between 23 and 36. The "frac1" (7) state is entered ten times in the trace sequence between 34 and 47. The traditional ITE approach never knows what event may occur next. Therefore, the design of an application must consider every possible event to call itself robust.

To enter the first operand "-3.14159" the ITE trace Table 8.0 below is shown in trace sequence 13 through to 48 where the subtraction operation is entered. In contrast the same functionality of entering "-3.14159" in the COSA Trace Table 8.1 below is accomplished between trace sequence 1 through to 10 where the same subtraction operation has been entered. There are 35 steps for ITE versus ten steps for COSA.

	State	Val		State	e→sig	Val		State	e→sig	Val
1	-calc		37	-frac1	2	-3.	73	-frac2	0	-2.
2	-calc		38	Frac1			74	-int2	0	-2.
3	-calc		39	-frac1	1	-3.	75	-int2	3	-2.
4	-ready		40	-frac1	1010	-3.	76	-frac2	2	-2.
5	-ready		41	-frac1	1010	-3.1	77	Frac2		
6	ready		42	-frac1	1010	-3.14	78	-frac2	1	-2.
7	-ready		43	-frac1	1010	-3.141	79	-frac2	1010	-2.
8	-begin		44	-frac1	1010	-3.1415	80	-frac2	1010	-2.1
9	-begin		45	-frac1	1107	-3.14159	81	-frac2	1010	-2.14
10	begin		46	-Oper1	1107	-3.14159	82	-frac2	1010	-2.141
11	-begin		47	-frac1	3	-3.14159	83	-frac2	1010	-2.1415
12	-begin		48	-opEnt	0	-3.14159	84	-frac2	1102	-2.14159
13	-negate1	0	49	-Oper1	0	-3.14159	85	-Oper2	1102	-2.14159
14	-begin,		50	-Oper1	3	-3.14159	86	-frac2	3	-2.14159
15	-calc,		51	-opEnt	2	-3.14159	87	-result	0	-2.14159
16	-begin,		52	opEnt			88	-Oper2	0	-2.14159
17	-ready		53	-opEnt	1	-3.14159	89	-ready	0	-2.14159
18	-ready		54	-opEnt	1107	-3.14159	90	-calc	0	-2.14159

---

[41] The "-"at the beginning of the method name indicates where I added trace to get this coverage.

19	-negate1	0		55	-negate2	0	0		91	-Oper2	3	-2.14159
20	negate1			56	-opEnt	0	0		92	-ready	2	-2.14159
21	-negate1	-0		57	-opEnt	3	0		93	ready		-2.14159
22	-negate1	-0		58	-negate2	2	0		94	-result	2	-2.14159
23	-int1	-3		59	negate2				95	result		-2.14159
24	-negate1	-3		60	-negate2	1	-0		96	-eval	1104	-2.14159
25	-Oper1	-3		61	-negate2	1010	-0		97	-result	1	-1
26	-calc			62	-int2	0	-2		98	-result	100	-1
27	-negate1	-3		63	-negate2	0	-2		99	-ready	100	-1
28	-Oper1	-3		64	-Oper2	0	-2		100	-calc	100	-1
29	Oper1			65	-calc	0			101	-result	3	-1
30	-int1	-3		66	-negate2	3	-2		102	ready	3	-1
31	int1			67	-Oper2	2	-2		103	final	0	-1
32	-int1	-3		68	Oper2				104	calc	0	-1
33	-int1	-3		69	-int2	2	-2		105	calc	3	-1
34	-frac1	-3.		70	int2				106	final	2	-1
35	-int1	-3.		71	-int2	1	-2		107	final	1	-1
36	-int1	-3.		72	-int2	1101	-2					

Table 8.0
ITE Calculator Trace

Starting in the ITE trace at 48 the subtraction operation is entered. To understand what was going on in the ITE approach the logic in the routines must be examined.

To handle the first operand there are eight "switch" statements, 33 "case" statements, and three "if" statements. The following shows the routine name followed by the number of "case" statements followed by the number of "if" statements:

procedure	"case"	"if"
"calc"	4	0
"ready"	6	0
"begin"	2	2
"negated1"	5	0
"int1"	4	0
"operand1"	3	0
"frac1"	4	0
"opentered"	5	1

For the subtraction operation there are three switch statements, thirteen case statements, and one if statement. The routines from trace 48 to trace 59 are:

procedure	"case"	"if"
"opentered"	5	1
"operand1"	3	0
"negated2"	5	0

At trace 59 the negation of the second operand is recognized. From trace 62 through to trace 90 where the "calc" routine is recognized and a result is created. The routines include:

procedure	"case"	"if"
"negated2"	5	0
"int2"	4	0
"operand2"	4	0
"calc"	4	0
"frac2"	3	0
"result"	1	0
"ready"	6	0

In the final result section there are seven "switch" statements, 27 "case" statements, and one "if" statement. The final result is produced at trace 97 and the application "unwinds" through trace 107.

That was a lot of logic to go through, but it truly illustrates the complexity of the ITE approach. With no temporal component, the ITE application must redundantly test to determine where it is executing because the application really does not know.

```
Date= 11/19/2018
Start of Calc-Tic-Tac-Toe Trace File.
True/False,   Dynamic,      Trace,      Result

T= 01; B= fNeg44,   Negate,      100 ; N=            -
T= 02; B= fDigit,   Any_Number, 101 ; N=           -3
T= 03;-B= fDigit,   Any_Number, 101 ; N=           -3
T= 04; B= fDot59,   One_Period, 102 ; N=          -3.
T= 05; B= fDigit,   Any_Number, 103 ; N=         -3.1
T= 06; B= fDigit,   Any_Number, 103 ; N=        -3.14
T= 07; B= fDigit,   Any_Number, 103 ; N=       -3.141
T= 08; B= fDigit,   Any_Number, 103 ; N=      -3.1415
T= 09; B= fDigit,   Any_Number, 103 ; N=     -3.14159
T= 10; B= fSub44,   Subtraction,501 ; N=
T= 11; B= fNeg44,   Negate,      700 ; N=            -
T= 12; B= fDigit,   Any_Number, 701 ; N=           -2
T= 13;-B= fDigit,   Any_Number, 701 ; N=           -2
T= 14; B= fDot59,   One_Period, 702 ; N=          -2.
T= 15; B= fDigit,   Any_Number, 703 ; N=         -2.1
T= 16; B= fDigit,   Any_Number, 703 ; N=        -2.14
T= 17; B= fDigit,   Any_Number, 703 ; N=       -2.141
T= 18; B= fDigit,   Any_Number, 703 ; N=      -2.1415
T= 19; B= fDigit,   Any_Number, 703 ; N=     -2.14159
T= 20; B= fEqual,   Equals,      901 ; N=           -1
```

Trace 8.1
Another COSA Calculator Trace

Temporal COSA knows exactly where it is always. The only testing required by COSA is a match between the dynamic state coming into the engine from an event and the static state that is predicted to be correct based on a prior knowledge of the Extended BNF Table design. The correct prediction is based on a temporal understanding of the logic that has been analyzed and designed into the COSA Extended BNF Table.

Examining more comparisons between the traditional ITE approach and COSA shows that the ITE calculator example written in C++ uses 112 "if" / "case" statements, has 577 lines of code in the logic, 694 lines of code in support of the logic, and 373 lines of code in the include files, for a total of 1,644 lines of code and has an overall complexity[42] of 195. The only caveat to this example is that Samek is introducing a "Quantum" architecture to state machines, which introduces some overhead.

The COSA calculator example uses one "if" / "case" statement, has 553 lines of code using Borland's v7.0 Delphi Environment and has an overall complexity of 57.   When the COSA calculator was implemented in C++ (Microsoft .NET 2003 Developer Studio), it had 527 lines of code.   The difference in size and complexity is a result of the COSA engineered software strategy where the engine is in temporal control and an orthogonal implementation is used for control-flow and data-flow.

The ITE spatial calculator used in this example was thoroughly designed, discussed, and published[43] as an example in another book. According to the SEI PowerPoint presentation[44], designed applications are smaller than if they had not been designed. The point here is that design is important, but architecture is critical. A temporal architecture like COSA makes a difference in the size of an application.

The following two columns compare the ITE procedures to the COSA procedures used in building the simple numbers in the calculator example.

__ITE Approach__	__COSA Approach__
23 lines of code in "negated1"	2 lines of code in "Negate"
5 case statements	
23 lines of code in "negated2"	
5 case statements	
17 lines of code in "operand1"	14 lines of code in "Any_Number"
3 case statements	
22 lines of code in "operand2"	
4 case statements	
16 lines of code in "zero1"	1 lines of code "Subtraction"
3 case statements	
16 lines of code in "zero2"	
3 case statements	

---

[42] CDOC Documentation Tool for C, C++ and Java, www.swbs.com and www.softwareblacksmiths.com using feature called CCALL™ caller/called hierarchy ("flow structure") between functions.
[43] Samek, Miro, PhD, *Practical Statecharts in C/C++*, CMP Books, © 2002.
[44] "PSP II-Designing and Verifying State Machines," Carnegie Mellon – Software Engineering Institute, February 2005, Slide Number 5.

16 lines of code in "int1"
>   4 case statements

16 lines of code in "int2"
>   4 case statements

12 lines of code in "frac1"   2 lines of code "One_Period"
>   3 case statements

12 lines of code in "frac2"
>   3 case statements

29 lines of code in "opEntered"   1 lines of code "Equals"
>   5 case statements

The number of "case" statements in an application indicates how state is understood in the ITE approach. The equivalent procedures in the COSA approach are only concerned about data manipulation; these procedures have nothing to do with logic.

8.3 Finding Reuse in ITE vs. COSA

The ability to find a way to reuse routines and logic is hampered by the intertwining logic and data manipulation in the ITE approach. Resulting in the logic design in the ITE approach having to create nearly duplicate routines "int1" and "int2", "negate1" and "negate2", "frac1" and "frac2", and "operand1" and "operand2".

When a developer is looking for routines to reuse, the spaghetti code approach of ITE in Figure 8.2 as compared to the simple flow of Figure 8.3, makes the choice easy. To reuse logic, routines, or components they must be easily understood. When a developer is looking for software to reuse it must have been well documented and fully understood. Most ITE software does not fall under that definition. Therefore, the developer must analyze the prospective reuse software for suitability. When analyzing COSA for reuse the specification, BNF Tree, Extended BNF Table, and procedures are all available and very simple. This makes COSA the best choice for reuse.

For a better understanding about reuse compare these two applications, side-by-side, with trace added. More than any other indicator, adding trace shows the difference between the traditional spatial approach and the temporal COSA approach. With COSA it is a matter of adding two lines of code to enable the two trace methods. Adding trace in the COSA application is easy. But when the same coverage of trace is added to the traditional approach it takes a significant amount of work. In this case it takes 15 lines of code spread throughout the application, increasing the chances of error. COSA produces simpler code, which is easier to develop, maintain, and reuse.

8.4 A Note on Static and Dynamic Trace

When ITE logic is scaled to large applications changes are extremely difficult to trace for change control documentation. Figure 8.3 is an application of about one thousand lines of code. Imagine what the call diagram looks like for larger applications with a million lines of code. Now add the ability through polymorphism and other mechanisms to dynamically change an application. The logic of ITE becomes even more complex. As a result, the logic becomes even more difficult to statically and dynamically trace.

8.5 An Ad Hoc Calculator

The previous comparisons between ITE and COSA are based on the architectural framework each espouses. For an additional comparison, an Ad Hoc ITE five-function calculator is created. Delphi was used because of its ability to rapidly create the prototype.

The creation of the four-function portion of the calculator was relatively easy. Saving the actual operation (for instance plus) until after the equal sign is clicked requires saving an operator state.

At this stage of its development the ad hoc approach looks clean. As other parts of the specifications are added the problem becomes more difficult. The negate function is now added using the subtract operator (remember no change sign key). With ITE this requires testing every section to see if the calculator is pre-operand or post-operate. Changing one piece of the logic requires all pieces to be reexamined.

At this point the code is "patchy" because of the additional state testing required to add the negate specification. However, when the multiplication of two negative numbers is tested the calculator fails. Code has to be added to handle negating the first operand differently from the second operand. The negation of the first operand occurs before a digit is entered. After the logic determines a number is not entered it must determine what happens next, operator or sign. The negation of the second operand occurs after the operator has been entered but before a digit is entered. The law of unintended consequences holds true. Once the multiply works the subtraction must be re-coded.

Next the percent function is added. Again, it is like adding a "patch" to a "patch" resulting in the additional testing of the code that was originally created to perform a different function. Once the percent is working the chain operation is tried and the calculator fails. The law of unintended consequences continues to hold true. Regression testing is starting to take on a life of its own.

The ITE Ad Hoc design now requires additional states to be added into working code to perform some additional function for which the original code was not intended. This next "patch" must determine if there is a pending operation with a first and second operation. State must be saved to allow for the completion of the operation or allow for the continuation of other operations. Somehow, this logic gets "fitted" into the existing logic without breaking what is working. This is a "patch" on a "patch" on a "patch", the essence of the problems with spatial software development. AND, the law of unintended consequences continues to hold true because of this spatial approach.

8.6 Summary

In examining the flow analysis of the procedure calls of COSA and traditional ITE, ITE is substantially more complex. When trace is used the comparison continues to illustrate the simplicity of coding in COSA.

COSA results in a highly predictable engineered approach to software. It is implemented as a state machine with a time component, inherent trace, robustness, and temporal logic reduces the complexity of software development. Adding logic or changing the way data is manipulated in COSA minimizes the law of unintended consequences.

Even a simple Ad Hoc calculator demonstrates how difficult it is to create clean logic with an ITE approach. The ad hoc calculator discussion in this chapter provides a good basis for understanding why software is difficult to implement and by comparison why COSA is truly revolutionary.

With the ITE approach to software, testing is extremely difficult because it is equally difficult to place any kind of metrics in the software. One of the problems in comparing the ITE approach to the power of COSA, is in providing the metrics in a way that is equal and complete. The Department of Commerce report produced by NIST[45] points out that software testing is just plain inadequate. The inherent structure of COSA significantly reduces the problems of software testing. The trace and structure lend access to automated tools able to analyze the application's structure from specification to final product resulting in a *COSA Temporal Engineering Certification* ™.

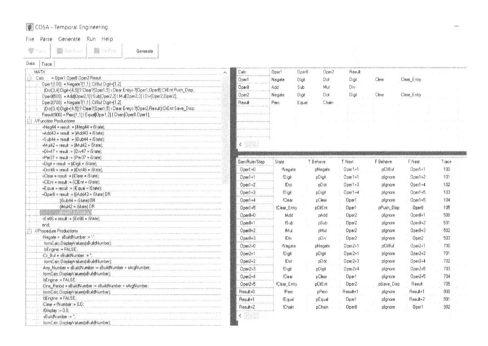

Figure 8.4 – 2018 Prototype COSA Matrix Generator

This prototype uses a BNF structure text file as input to generate the calculator table, functions, and procedures. The BNF from the upper left corner and here:

:Calc = Oper1 Oper8 Oper2 Result;

Oper1(100) = Negate?[1,1]::ClrBuf Digit+[1,2] (Dot[3,4] Digit+[4,5])?

   (Clear?[Oper1,5] <Clear Entry>?[Oper1,Oper8]:ClrEnt:Push_Disp;

Oper8(500) = Add[Oper2,1] | Sub[Oper2,2] | Mul[Oper2,3] | Div[Oper2,Oper2];

Oper2(700) = Negate?[1,1]::ClrBuf Digit+[1,2] (Dot[3,4] Digit+[4,5])?

   Clear?[Oper1,5] <Clear Entry>?[Oper2,Result]:ClrEnt:Save_Disp;

Result(900) = Perc[1,1] | Equal[Oper1,2] | Chain[Oper8,Oper1];

---

[45] Gregory Tassey, "The Economic Impacts of Inadequate Infrastructure for Software Testing", May 2002, National Institute of Standards and Technology.

Chapter 9
Robot Arm Logic – in 3D

With Temporal Engineering common sense says that creating a Robot Arm should not be complex. Common sense is right. There are four triangles that must be solved in moving the robot arms to a target.

> S – Shoulder; E – Elbow; W – Wrist; Fingertip – FT; T – Target;
> A – Arm; F – Forearm; H – Hand;

1) The solution-triangle involves the sides:

a= Angle S-FT to the T top-down view
b= Angle S-E to T
c= Angle E-W to T
d= Angle W-FT to T

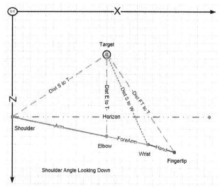

Figure 9.0

The first triangle is the top view at right is the down-looking Z-X axis. This angle moves the entire arm CCW or CW.

2) The second triangle is the Arm and Forearm, the 'Dist S to W' represents the solution when the arm has been moved to the target. The final solution-triangle is used to determine when the robot's arms are moving in the right direction and eventually have been moved to the proper positions and if the arm can   reach the robot.

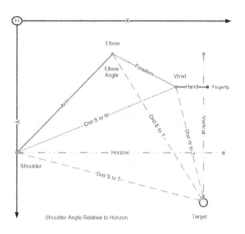

Figure 9.1

3) The third triangle is defined by the Arm, 'Dist E to T', and 'Dist S to T'. The Dist E to T (DE2T) is used as one of the measures to ensure that the motion is toward the target. The Dist S to T (DS2T) does not change with a stationary target but would change in a chasing target scenario.

4) The final triangle is defined by Dist W to T, Wrist, and Dist FT to T. This final triangle is used to move the hand into a grasp position relative to the target.

The robot uses a ping to determine the target position. The ping measurement returns distance Dist S to T (DS2T) and the Dist E to T (DE2T). The cosine rule is used to determine the solution angle; that is, the angles the robot's arms will make at the final position with the target.

The first rule determines if the target can be reached by determining the azimuth for the quadrant. The second rule moves the Arm to the solution angle for the shoulder. The third rule moves the Forearm to the target angle defined by the solution angle for the elbow. The forth rule moves the hand into a horizontal position beneath the target in a position to grasp.

9.1 The sum of the internal angles equals 180°

$A + B + C = 180°$
Shoulder Angle + Target Angle + Elbow Angle = 180°

Initially none of the angles are know so the cosine rule must be solved for each angle. The distances are based on information the robot receives from its ping measurement and the length of the appendages are defined in the robot's properties.

Figure 12.2 shows the geometry for the 3-D aspect of the shoulder angle using ping.

9.2 The 'cosine rule' is defined as:

$a^2 = b^2 + c^2 - 2bc\ cosA;$

The cosine rule applied to the robot shoulder angle:

$4Arm^2 = S2T^2 + ArmLen^2 - (2 * S2T * ArmLen)* cos\ shldr;$
Solution Angles
$DE2T^2 = S2T^2 + ArmLen^2 - (2 * S2T * ArmLen)* cos\ shldr;$
Starting Angles
$Cos(shldr) =(S2T^2 + ArmLen^2 - DE2T^2)/(2 * S2T * ArmLen)$

In the program the **shoulder angle** in degrees uses PING to get distances to the target is coded as:

```
rTemp1 := (rShldrDist*rShldrDist) + (rArmLen * rArmLen) −
        (rElbowDist * rElbowDist);
rTemp2 := (2.0 * rShldrDist * rArmLen);
rShldrAngle := ArcCos(rTemp1/ rTemp2) * (57.29582791;
```

The program calculates the shoulder **solution angle** in degrees is coded as:

```
rTemp1 := (r4ArmLen * r4ArmLen) + (rArmLen * rArmLen) −
        (rShldrDist*rShldrDist);
rTemp2 := (2.0 * rArmLen * rShldrDist)
rShldrAngle := ArcCos(rTemp1/rTemp2) * 57.29582791;

using rArmLen = 240; r4ArmLen = 100; and rShldrDist = 240;
rTemp1 = 10,000;    rTemp2 = 115,200
cosine(rTemp1/rTemp2) = 0.08680556 - in degrees 85.02
```

9.3 When applied to robot elbow angle back to shoulder and wrist:

$b^2 = a^2 + c^2 - 2ac\ cosB$
$S2T^2 = 4Arm^2 + Arm^2 -2 * 4Arm * Arm * cos\ elbow;$ Solution Angle
$S2T^2 = 4Arm^2 + Arm^2 -2 * 4Arm * Arm * cos\ elbow;$ Starting Angle

$Cos\ elbow = (4Arm^2 + Arm^2 - S2T^2)/(2 * 4Arm * Arm)$

9.4 When applied to robot wrist angle looking back to shoulder and elbow:

$c^2 = b^2 + a^2 - 2ba\ cosC$
$Arm^2 = S2T^2 + 4Arm^2 - cos\ wrist;$ Solution Angle
$Arm^2 = S2T^2 + DE2T^2 - cos\ wrist;$ Starting Angles

In the program the **starting angle** in degrees is coded as:

rTemp1:=(rElbowDist *rElbowDist)+(rArmLen*rArmLen)–(rS2WDist*rS2WDist);
rElbowAngle := ArcCos(rTemp1/(2.0 * rElbowDist * rArmLen))* 57.29582791;

and in the program the **solution angle** in degrees is coded as:

rTemp1 := (r4ArmLen*r4ArmLen)+(rArmLen*rArmLen)–(rShldrDist*rShldrDist);

rElbowAngle := ArcCos(rTemp1/(2.0 * r4ArmLen * rArmLen))* 57.29582791;

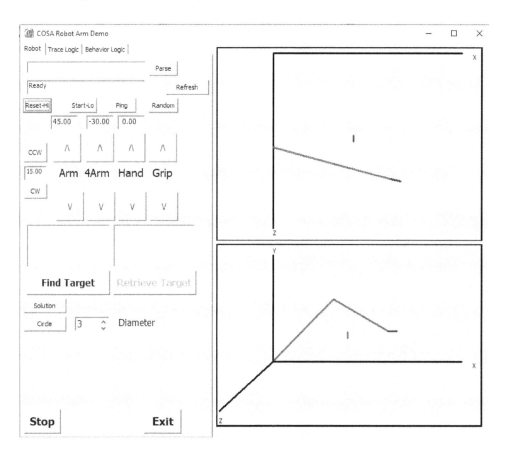

Figure 9.2
Robot Arm Simulation

In this chapter I will develop the logic associated with a robot arm simulation in three-dimensions. The logic example shows the automated find the target application.

The logic definition starts with BNF view of what robot arm looks like:

RobotArm = Shoulder Arm 4Arm Hand;

The initial definition is really very simple. But as you can expect the behavior of the arm will add a significant amount of complexity. The Arm moves at a shoulder joint and the 4Arm and Hand must move together with the Arm. We represent the Arm movement as up or down. If the Arm moves, then the 4Arm and Hand must also move. The initial Arm definition looks like this:

Arm = (Up | Down) 4Arm Hand;

This is read as move Arm up or down then move 4Arm then move Hand; The same consideration must be taken for the wrist relationship between the 4Arm and Hand. If the elbow of the 4Arm moves, then the wrist Hand relationship must move along too. This relationship is expressed as:

4Arm = (Up | Down) Hand;

The Hand at this point does not have any other relationships ignoring the complexity of grasp. The Hand definition is simple:

Hand = (Up | Down);

The robot arm logic looks like this for now:

RobotArm = Shoulder Arm 4Arm Hand;
Arm = (Up | Down) 4Arm Hand;
4Arm = (Up | Down) Hand;
Hand = (Up | Down);

The Shoulder view is the third dimension. Using a top-down view of the Z-X axis the Arm as a unit moves Counter Clockwise (CCW) or Clockwise (CW). The Solution-Angle is formed by the side S-FT and the side S to T. A positive angle means the T is to the left or CCW to the FT. A negative angle would require a right or CW motion to align with the T.

The Arm movements now requires further definitions. The ArmUp definition includes direction and the other relationships:

> ArmUp = Up ClearArm MoveArm Move4Arm MoveHand;
> Up = SetAngleInc +1; // move up one degree

Moving the Arm down requires the same relationships to be followed in the opposite direction:

> ArmDown = Down ClearArm MoveArm Move4Arm MoveHand;
> Down = SetAngleDec -1;   // move down one degree

This logic allows the Arm, 4Arm, and Hand to move up and down together as a unit.

9.5 The 4Arm Logic

A pattern of logic has been established at this point. From the logic of the Arm we can expect to have five similar steps. The difference being that the 4Arm does not need to manage the Arm other than to follow the elbow joint. To move the 4Arm up the logic looks like this:

> 4ArmUp = Up ClearArm DrawArm Move4Arm MoveHand;
> Up = SetAngleInc +1; // move up one degree

Notice that the logic is very similar to the Arm logic. The difference is in the DrawArm rather than MoveArm since only the 4Arm and Hand are moving. To move the 4Arm down the logic looks like this:

> 4ArmDown = Down ClearArm DrawArm Move4Arm MoveHand;
> Down = SetAngleDec -1;   // move down one degree

This is the complete logic allowing the 4Arm and Hand to move together as a unit.

9.6 The Hand Logic

The pattern of logic continues. As you might expect the only differences in the Hand logic will be in drawing the Arm and 4Arm, not moving them.

> HandUp = Up ClearArm DrawArm Draw4Arm MoveHand;
> Up = SetAngleInc +1;
> HandDown = Down ClearArm DrawArm Draw4Arm MoveHand;
> Down = SetAngleDec -1;

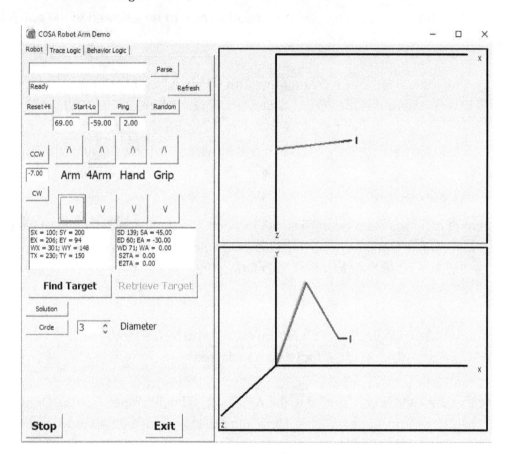

Figure 9.3
Robot Hand Near Target

9.7 The Robot Arm Logic Table

The logic is complete and implemented in a table show below. In my implementation the Arm, 4Arm, and Hand were implemented as objects. The procedures in the table provide no additional logic. There is only one if statement in this portion of the robot arm simulation and that is in the engine.

```
procedure TCOSAbehavior.CreateRules(formRobot : TformRobot);
begin
{$include Behavior_Data.inc}
//                  Static        True           Next True   False        Next False
//       Rules      State         Behavior       Rule        Behavior Rule              Trace
   pBRT(rBehave,    fSearch,      Ignore,        rSearch,    Ignore,  rBehave+ ,  1000);
   pBRT(rBehave+ ,  fRetrev,      Ignore,        rRtreve,    Ignore,  rError,     1001);
//==================================================================================
//         Find Target
//==================================================================================
pBRT(rSearch,     fPing,          Ignore,        rSearch+ , Ignore,  rSearch+ ,  1000);
   // can the arm reach the target?
pBRT(rSearch+ ,   fArmReach,      pNotReach,     rError,    Ignore,  rSearch+ ,  1201);
   // find Azimuth target is in
pBRT(rSearch+ ,   fAzimuth1,      pSetAz1,       rSearch+ , Ignore,  rSearch+ ,  1202);
pBRT(rSearch+ ,   fAzimuth1,      pTopSolnAdd,   rSearch+ , Ignore,  rSearch+ ,  1203);
pBRT(rSearch+ ,   fAzimuth2,      pSetAz2,       rSearch+ , Ignore,  rSearch+ ,  1203);
pBRT(rSearch+ ,   fAzimuth2,      pTopSolnSub,   rSearch+ , Ignore,  rSearch+ ,  1203);
pBRT(rSearch+ ,   fAzimuth3,      pSetAz3,       rSearch+ , Ignore,  rSearch+ ,  1204);
pBRT(rSearch+ ,   fAzimuth4,      pSetAz4,       rSearch+ , Ignore,  rError,     1205);
   // find quadrant target is in
pBRT(rSearch+ ,   fQuad1,         pSetQd1,       rArm,      Ignore,  rSearch+ ,  1200);
pBRT(rSearch+ ,   fQuad2,         pSetQd2,       rArm,      Ignore,  rSearch+ ,  1201);
pBRT(rSearch+ ,   fQuad3,         pSetQd3,       rArm,      Ignore,  rSearch+ ,  1202);
pBRT(rSearch+ ,   fQuad4,         pSetQd4,       rArm,      Ignore,  rError,     1203);
//----------------------------------------------------------------------------------
```

Figure 9.4

The robot arms are controlled with the buttons in the simulator. In Figure 9.3 the buttons were used to move the Hand close to the target for gripping.

9.8 Automatically Finding a Target

I continued developing this robot arm to automatically find a target. For any robot to find a target it must first be able to sense where the target is located. A ping using some part of the frequency spectrum or static passive receiver is used in commercial robots. In this example I decided to use an active ping source from the shoulder, the elbow, and the wrist joints. In a two-dimensional space using three ping sources I can find my target and move the robot arm to the target. In the three-space the angle to the target from the shoulder facing also needs to be determined and changed, as necessary.

This matrix is determining which quadrant the target is in relative to the elbow.

```
//----------------------------------------------------------------------
// Target angles relative to shoulder angle
// Elbow distance to target should be about the length of the 4Arm
pBRT(rArm,       fE1Ping,     Ignore,    rArm+1,    Ignore,    rArm+4,    2000);
pBRT(rArm+1,     fEAPing,     pMvAUp,    rArm+3,    Ignore,    rArm+2,    2010);
pBRT(rArm+2,     fECPing,     pMvADn,    rArm+3,    Ignore,    rArm+3,    2020);
pBRT(rArm+3,     fProxArm,    Ignore,    r4Arm,     Ignore,    rArm,      2030);

pBRT(rArm+4,     fE2Ping,     Ignore,    rArm+5,    Ignore,    rArm+8,    2040);
pBRT(rArm+5,     fEAPing,     pMvAUp,    rArm+7,    Ignore,    rArm+6,    2050);
pBRT(rArm+6,     fECPing,     pMvADn,    rArm+7,    Ignore,    rArm+7,    2060);
pBRT(rArm+7,     fProxArm,    Ignore,    r4Arm,     Ignore,    rArm+4,    2070);

pBRT(rArm+8,     fE3Ping,     Ignore,    rArm+9,    Ignore,    rArm+12,   2080);
pBRT(rArm+9,     fEAPing,     pMvADn,    rArm+11,   Ignore,    rArm+10,   2090);
pBRT(rArm+10,    fECPing,     pMvAUp,    rArm+11,   Ignore,    rArm+11,   2100);
pBRT(rArm+11,    fProxArm,    Ignore,    r4Arm,     Ignore,    rArm+8,    2110);

pBRT(rArm+12,    fE4Ping,     Ignore,    rArm+13,   Ignore,    r4Arm,     2120);
pBRT(rArm+13,    fEAPing,     pMvADn,    rArm+15,   Ignore,    rArm+14,   2130);
pBRT(rArm+14,    fECPing,     pMvAUp,    rArm+15,   Ignore,    rArm+15,   2140);
pBRT(rArm+15,    fProxArm,    Ignore,    r4Arm,     Ignore,    rArm+12,   2150);
// Move Elbow DOWN to get to 4Arm distance
//======================================================================
```

Figure 9.5

Once the Arm logic is positioned correctly the Forearm begins to move.

The Forearm searchs looking to see if there is proximity to the Wrist at r4Arm + 3 returning to r4Arm to continue moving toward the target. When proximity is determined the r4Arm+3 transitions to rFound.

These four groups are quadrant oriented Q1, Q2, Q3, and Q4, relative to the Wrist in the same sense that the previous Elbow was determing its respective target quadrant. You can see the top rule in each group goes to the next group on a false first ping to determine which quadrant the target is located.

```
// Elbow
//=============================================================
// determine if the target is above or below hand
pBRT(r4Arm,      fW1Ping,     Ignore,    r4Arm+1,   Ignore,   r4Arm+4,   2300);
pBRT(r4Arm+1,    fWAPing,     pMv4AUp,   r4Arm+3,   Ignore,   r4Arm+2,   2310);
pBRT(r4Arm+2,    fWCPing,     pMv4ADn,   r4Arm+3,   Ignore,   r4Arm+3,   2320);
pBRT(r4Arm+3,    fProxWrst,   Ignore,    rFound,    Ignore,   r4Arm,     2330);

pBRT(r4Arm+4,    fW2Ping,     Ignore,    r4Arm+5,   Ignore,   r4Arm+8,   2340);
pBRT(r4Arm+5,    fWAPing,     pMv4AUp,   r4Arm+7,   Ignore,   r4Arm+6,   2350);
pBRT(r4Arm+6,    fWCPing,     pMv4ADn,   r4Arm+7,   Ignore,   r4Arm+7,   2360);
pBRT(r4Arm+7,    fProxWrst,   Ignore,    rFound,    Ignore,   r4Arm+4,   2370);

pBRT(r4Arm+8,    fW3Ping,     Ignore,    r4Arm+9,   Ignore,   r4Arm+12,  2380);
pBRT(r4Arm+9,    fWAPing,     pMv4ADn,   r4Arm+11,  Ignore,   r4Arm+10,  2390);
pBRT(r4Arm+10,   fWCPing,     pMv4AUp,   r4Arm+11,  Ignore,   r4Arm+11,  2400);
pBRT(r4Arm+11,   fProxWrst,   Ignore,    rFound,    Ignore,   r4Arm+8,   2410);

pBRT(r4Arm+12,   fW4Ping,     Ignore,    r4Arm+13,  Ignore,   rDone,     2420);
pBRT(r4Arm+13,   fWAPing,     pMv4ADn,   r4Arm+15,  Ignore,   r4Arm+14,  2430);
pBRT(r4Arm+14,   fWCPing,     pMv4AUp,   r4Arm+15,  Ignore,   r4Arm+15,  2440);
pBRT(r4Arm+15,   fProxWrst,   Ignore,    rFound,    Ignore,   r4Arm+12,  2450);
// Target is below hand move forearm up
//=============================================================
```

Figure 9.6

With the Arm and Forearm in the correct position the Hand is in proximity to determine if a grasp is possible.

```
//=============================================================
// The target should be at the grasp of the hand
pBRT(rHand,      fMvHandUp,   Ignore,    rHand+1,   Ignore,   rHand+1,   2750);
pBRT(rHand+1,    fFPing,      Ignore,    rHand+2,   Ignore,   rHand+2,   2751);
pBRT(rHand+2,    fFCloser,    Ignore,    rHand+3,   Ignore,   rHand+6,   2752);
// Target is above hand grasp up
pBRT(rHand+3,    fMvHandUp,   Ignore,    rHand+4,   Ignore,   rHand+4,   2753);
pBRT(rHand+4,    fFPing,      Ignore,    rHand+5,   Ignore,   rHand+5,   2754);
pBRT(rHand+5,    fFAngLE0,    Ignore,    rFound,    Ignore,   rHand+3,   2755);
// Target is below hand grasp down
pBRT(rHand+6,    fMvHandDn,   Ignore,    rHand+7,   Ignore,   rHand+7,   2756);
pBRT(rHand+7,    fFPing,      Ignore,    rHand+8,   Ignore,   rHand+8,   2757);
pBRT(rHand+8,    fFAngLE0,    Ignore,    rFound,    Ignore,   rHand+6,   2758);
pBRT(rHand+9,    fProxFngr,   Ignore,    rFound,    Ignore,   rHand,     2759);
//=============================================================
//       Retrieve Target
//=============================================================
pBRT(rRtreve,    fFound,      Ignore,    rRtreve+1, pSearch,  rDone,     2900);
//=============================================================
//       Draw a circle
//=============================================================
pBRT(rCircle+0,  fPing,       Ignore,    rCircle+1, Ignore,   rCircle+1, 3000);
pBRT(rCircle+1,  fCircleTop,  Ignore,    rDone,     Ignore,   rCircle+2, 3010);
// found
pBRT(rFound,     fFound,      pFound,    rDone,     Ignore,   rError,    9984);
// Done
pBRT(rDone,      fDone,       pDone,     rDone,     Ignore,   rError,    9985);
// Error
pBRT(rError,     fError,      pError,    rError,    Ignore,   rError,    9986);
```

Figure 9.7

9.9 Heuristic Behaviors

The ability to find objects of specific types is a learned behavior. The ability to distinguish can result from the information returned in the Ping. Color spectrum, size, and some aspects of the material can easily be determined by the Ping spectrum. Distinguishing the difference between a wire, battery, light, and an LED requires more ability than just the ping spectrum. The detailed physical characteristics would need to be provided as a learned basis that can be used for comparison.

This section uses a command line parser to ask the Robot to determine which object is being asked for by the operator.

```
//                    Static      True        Next True   False      Next False
//      Rules         State       Behavior    Rule        Behavior   Rule        Trace
pSYN(rsFind,          fsFind,     synMatch,   rsSpat,     Ignore,    rsFind+1,   7000);
pSYN(rsFind+1,        fsSearch,   synMatch,   rsSpat,     Ignore,    rsAct,      7001);

pSYN(rsAct,           fsCut,      synMatch,   rsSpat,     Ignore,    rsAct+1,    7010);
pSYN(rsAct+1,         fsGrab,     synMatch,   rsSpat,     Ignore,    rsSpat,     7011);

pSYN(rsSpat,          fsNearest,  synMatch,   rsSize,     Ignore,    rsSpat+1,   7020);
pSYN(rsSpat+1,        fsFarest,   synMatch,   rsSize,     Ignore,    rsSize,     7021);

pSYN(rsSize,          fsSmall,    synMatch,   rsColor,    Ignore,    rsSize+1,   7040);
pSYN(rsSize+1,        fsLarge,    synMatch,   rsColor,    Ignore,    rsColor,    7041);

pSYN(rsColor,         fsRed,      synMatch,   rsSize,     Ignore,    rsColor+1,  7030);
pSYN(rsColor+1,       fsYellow,   synMatch,   rsSize,     Ignore,    rsColor+2,  7031);
pSYN(rsColor+2,       fsBlue,     synMatch,   rsSize,     Ignore,    rsColor+3,  7032);
pSYN(rsColor+3,       fsGreen,    synMatch,   rsSize,     Ignore,    rsObj,      7033);

pSYN(rsObj,           fsWire,     synMatch,   rsSColon,   Ignore,    rsObj+1,    7050);
pSYN(rsObj+1,         fsBattery,  synMatch,   rsSColon,   Ignore,    rsObj+2,    7051);
pSYN(rsObj+2,         fsLight,    synMatch,   rsSColon,   Ignore,    rsObj+3,    7052);
pSYN(rsObj+3,         fsLED,      synMatch,   rsSColon,   pObjErr,   rsCirc,     7053);

pSYN(rsCirc,          fsCirc,     pDrawCirc,  rsCirc+1,   Ignore,    rsRect,     7060);
pSYN(rsCirc+1,        fsCirc,     pDrawCirc,  rsCirc+2,   Ignore,    rsCirc+2,   7061);
pSYN(rsCirc+2,        fsCirc,     pDrawCirc,  rsSColon,   Ignore,    rsRect,     7062);

pSYN(rsRect,          fsRect,     synMatch,   rsRect,     Ignore,    rsRect+1,   7070);
pSYN(rsRect+1,        fsWire,     synMatch,   rsRect,     Ignore,    rsRect+2,   7071);
pSYN(rsRect+2,        fsWire,     synMatch,   rsRect,     Ignore,    rsSqr,      7072);

pSYN(rsSqr,           fsSqr,      synMatch,   rsSqr,      Ignore,    rsSqr+1,    7080);
pSYN(rsSqr+1,         fsWire,     synMatch,   rsSqr,      Ignore,    rsSqr+2,    7081);
pSYN(rsSqr+2,         fsWire,     synMatch,   rsSqr,      Ignore,    rsSColon,   7082);

pSYN(rsSColon,        fsSColon,   EndofCmnd,  rsFind,     pTermErr,  rsFind,     7090);

pSYN(rsSynErr,        fsEnd,      synMatch,   rsSynErr+1, Ignore,    rsSynErr+1, 7086);
pSYN(rsSynErr+1,      fsEnd,      synMatch,   rsSynErr+2, Ignore,    rsSynErr+2, 7087);
pSYN(rsSynEnd,        fsEnd,      synMatch,   rsFind,     Ignore,    rsFind,     7088);
```

Figure 9.8

For example, the operator could ask for "Grab Red Battery" and the Robot would begin the logic of determining if there was such an object within reach.

//	Static	True	Next True	False	Next False	
// Rules	State	Behavior	Rule	Behavior	Rule	Trace
pPAR(rFind,	fFind,	parMatch,	rAct,	Ignore,	rFind+,	);
pPAR(rFind+,	fSearch,	parMatch,	rAct,	Ignore,	rAct,	);
pPAR(rAct,	fCut,	parMatch,	rSpat,	Ignore,	rAct+,	);
pPAR(rAct+,	fGrab,	parMatch,	rSpat,	Ignore,	rSpat,	);
pPAR(rSpat,	fNearest,	parMatch,	rColor,	Ignore,	rSpat+,	);
pPAR(rSpat+,	fFarthest,	parMatch,	rColor,	Ignore,	rColor,	);
pPAR(rColor,	fRed,	parMatch,	rSize,	Ignore,	rColor+,	);
pPAR(rColor+,	fYellow,	parMatch,	rSize,	Ignore,	rColor+,	);
pPAR(rColor+,	fBlue,	parMatch,	rSize,	Ignore,	rColor+,	);
pPAR(rColor+,	fGreen,	parMatch,	rSize,	Ignore,	rSize,	);
pPAR(rSize,	fSmall,	parMatch,	rObj,	Ignore,	rSize+,	);
pPAR(rSize+,	fLarge,	parMatch,	rObj,	Ignore,	rObj,	);
pPAR(rObj,	fWire,	parMatch,	rParEnd,	Ignore,	rObj+,	);
pPAR(rObj+,	fBattery,	parMatch,	rParEnd,	Ignore,	rObj+,	);
pPAR(rObj+,	fLight,	parMatch,	rParEnd,	Ignore,	rObj+,	);
pPAR(rObj+,	fLED,	parMatch,	rParEnd,	Ignore,	rCirc,	);
pPAR(rCirc+,	fCirc,	parMatch,	rFind,	Ignore,	rRect,	);
pPAR(rCirc+,	fLED,	parMatch,	rCirc+,	Ignore,	rCirc+,	);
pPAR(rCirc+,	fLED,	parMatch,	rCirc+,	Ignore,	rCirc+,	);
pPAR(rRect+,	fRect,	parMatch,	rRect+,	Ignore,	rSqr,	);
pPAR(rRect+,	fLED,	parMatch,	rRect+,	Ignore,	rRect+,	);
pPAR(rRect+,	fLED,	parMatch,	rRect+,	Ignore,	rRect+,	);
pPAR(rSqr+,	fSqr,	parMatch,	rSqr+,	Ignore,	rParEnd,	);
pPAR(rSqr+,	fLED,	parMatch,	rSqr+,	Ignore,	rSqr+,	);
pPAR(rSqr+,	fLED,	parMatch,	rSqr+,	Ignore,	rSqr+,	);
pPAR(rParEnd,	fEnd,	parMatch,	rFind,	Ignore,	rFind,	);

Figure 9.9

Once the target has been located the logic can begin to move the robot arm toward the target. Developing the BNF logic for this application is a little more complex but it builds on the previous Robot Arm logic.

Find Target = Search;

Three pings have been sent looking for distance and angles. With the ping information the determination must be made if the hand can reach the target. If the distance from the shoulder joint to the target is greater than the Hand can reach, then the target cannot be acquired. The Robot Arm knows all of the angles of its joints, so this calculation is straightforward to determine if the target is in range.

Search = GetFDistance then GetEDistance then GetWDistance;

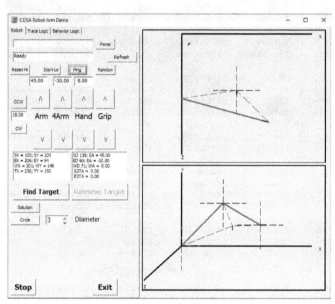

Figure 9.10
Robot Arm Pinging Target

Once these distances are known the Arm moves to its acceptable distance. Then the Forearm moves to its acceptable distance. Then the Wrist determines if the object is in the range to be grasped. If the target has moved this process is completed with each calculation the result of a Ping. When the proximity is correct the target is grasped, and the process stops.

All these calculations could go on in parallel. All the robot's limbs could be moving in parallel. The coordination would require communication to ensure that a potential grasp is possible. One of the issues that must be checked with each ping is the condition of the target getting too close for a grasp. If the random generation of the target is near the shoulder and the Forearm and Hand cannot reach the target, then the robot must move away from the target in order for the distance to the target to fall in that "Goldie Locks" range where the target can be grasped.

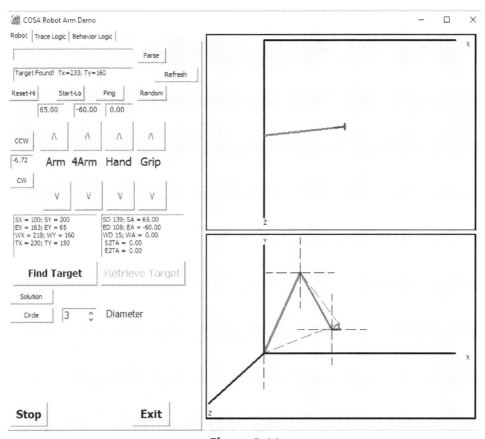

Figure 9.11
Automated Logic Found Target

Notice in the Z view the arm is shorter. That is because the arm at the elbow has contracted so the arm looks shorter from above. In reality the arm is the same length.

```
{$INCLUDE 'Create_Data.inc'}
//                Static    True            Next True    False        Next False
//     Rules      State     Behavior        Rule         Behavior     Rule         Trace
// Arm1 Operations
   pBRT(rArmUp,    iUp,     ArrowUp,        rArmUp+1,    Ignore,      rArmDn,       300);
   pBRT(rArmUp+1,  iUp,     RotArm,         rArmUp+2,    Ignore,      rError,       301);
   pBRT(rArmUp+2,  iUp,     Mov4Arm,        rArmUp+3,    Ignore,      rError,       302);
   pBRT(rArmUp+3,  iUp,     MovHand,        rArmUp,      Ignore,      rError,       303);
// 4
   pBRT(rArmDn,    iDn,     ArrowDn,        rArmDn+1,    Ignore,      rArmUp,       504);
   pBRT(rArmDn+1,  iDn,     RotArm,         rArmDn+2,    Ignore,      rError,       505);
   pBRT(rArmDn+2,  iDn,     Mov4Arm,        rArmDn+3,    Ignore,      rError,       506);
   pBRT(rArmDn+3,  iDn,     MovHand,        rArmDn,      Ignore,      rError,       507);
// 4- Forarm Arm2 Operations
   pBRT(rForUp,    iUp,     ArrowUp,        rForUp+1,    Ignore,      rForDn,       708);
   pBRT(rForUp+1,  iUp,     Rot4Arm,        rForUp+2,    Ignore,      rError,       709);
   pBRT(rForUp+2,  iUp,     MovHand,        rForUp,      Ignore,      rError,       710);
// 3
   pBRT(rForDn,    iDn,     ArrowDn,        rForDn+1,    Ignore,      rForUp,       911);
   pBRT(rForDn+1,  iDn,     Rot4Arm,        rForDn+2,    Ignore,      rError,       912);
   pBRT(rForDn+2,  iDn,     MovHand,        rForDn,      Ignore,      rError,       913);
// 3
   pBRT(rHandUp,   iUp,     ArrowUp,        rHandUp+1,   Ignore,      rHandUp+1,    1114);
   pBRT(rHandUp+1, iUp,     RotHand,        rHandUp,     Ignore,      rHandUp+1,    1115);
// 2
   pBRT(rHandDn,   iDn,     ArrowDn,        rHandDn+1,   Ignore,      rError,       1116);
   pBRT(rHandDn+1, iDn,     RotHand,        rHandDn,     Ignore,      rError,       1117);
// 2
   pBRT(rGripUp,   iUp,     HandOpen,       rGripUp,     Ignore,      rGripUp+1,    1118);
// 1
   pBRT(rGripDn,   iDn,     HandClose,      rGripDn,     Ignore,      rError,       1119);
// 1
   pBRT(rError,    0,       pError,         rStop,       pError,      rStop,        9986);
// 1
   pBRT(rStop,     0,       pStop,          rStop,       pError,      rStop,        9999);
```

Figure 9.12

Search-Locate Behavior Logic

9.10 Summary

Every aspect of this robot arm was defined using rules. I cannot imagine the complexity of trying to do this with the traditional if-then-else approach.

Chapter 10
Data Migration

The extract-translate-load (ETL) process is SRC → XLATE → DST. It is a fairly straightforward temporal process. The problems lie in the different structures and data type implementations of the various vendors. There are also inconsistencies within a vendor. One would think that it would be straightforward and consistent when extracting an Access database and loading the extraction into an identical Access database. But it is not. Some of the data types are inconsistent as we shall see.

This section of the book does not get into the code detail because it would make the book very large and boring. This section is to show all the Temporal Engineering logic associated with each of the steps in creating an ETL tool. My experience comes from having implemented a number of UNIX based commercial ETL tools using Oracle PL/SQL as the database interface.

10.1 ETL Process Buttons – Step by Step

I wanted to make this easy to use with very little training and documentation. This app uses a number along with enabling buttons to indicate what process can be started next. As of this writing there are seventeen steps. The BNF design begins with the first sentence of this chapter. That is:

ETL = Extract XLATE Load;

The Extract consists of

Extract = SRC Connect DST Connect.

The SRC Connect definition consist of:

SRC Connect = Select SRC Type Select DST Type Find SRC ODBC Make SRC Connection Extract SRC Schema;

The process consists of the following steps:

1 – Select Source Type Data Vendor or Type
2 – Select Destination Type Data Vendor or Type
3 – Find the SRC ODBC connections
4 – Select one of the SRC ODBC connections
5 – Make the SRC Connection
6 – Extract the SRC Schema

The SRC side is complete. The DST Connection side consists of the following: Find DST ODBC Make DST Connection Extract DST Schema;

7 – Find the DST ODBC connections
8 – Select one of the DST ODBC connections
9 – Make the DST Connection
10 – Extract the DST Schema

The DST Connection side is complete.

The following are optional depending on what translations have been made in the mapping area and the status of the destination schema.

XLATE = (Load Map File? | Map SRC Schema to DST Schema?) (Drop All DST Tables?) Copy Map Defined to DST Schema? Create DST Schema from Mapping Tree? Load DST Database;

11 – Load Map File (Optional) Created from a previous session.

or

12 – Map SRC schema to the DST schema (Optional)
13 – Drop All Tables (Optional) To be recreated from mapping.

14 – Table Type Corrections (Automated based on type mapping)
15 – Copy Map defined schema to DST Schema (Optional)
16 – Create Schema (DST Optional) from the mapping tree.
17 – Load (DST) database

All the following actions will be shown in screenshots in the next chapter. These seventeen actions will complete the ETL process. As the ETL progresses status is provided in the status bar at the bottom of the GUI and trace information is provide on the Tab Page labeled "Trace".

The connection types, Step 1 and 2, are listed on their own tab window. The Step 3-Source and Step 7-Destination buttons provide a list of the ODBC connections available on the system. The list for each is located at the bottom of the GUI in their respective list boxes. The 4 & 8 Select functions are performed for each Source and Destination by clicking on one of the ODBC connections in their respective list box.

The 5-Connect SRC and 9-Connect DST will use the selected ODBC definitions to make the connection. Failures are reported in the status bar along with trace information on the Trace Page. The 6 & 10 Schema extractions pull the respective schemas into a tree format for viewing. A map file can then be reloaded using 11 – Load from File. The 12 – Copy SRC to Map button copies the SRC schema into the MAP tree in the center of the application. In the MAP tree the schema can be modified and saved in a Map Schema file.

The 13 – Drop All Tables button drops the DST schema. Step 14 – Uses rules based on known data type anomalies. The 15 – Copy Map – DST places the new schema in the DST tree allowing the 16 – Create DST Schema button to create a new schema for loading. The final Step 17 – Load button, loads the destination connection with the data from the source connection based on the rules created in the mapping.

The data migration application is implemented as a non-trivial hierarchical state machine. The application consists of the GUI application class from which the subordinate state machines are derived. There are two sides and middle to this application: the source side, the translation, and the destination. The two sides use ODBC connection to attach to their respective targets.

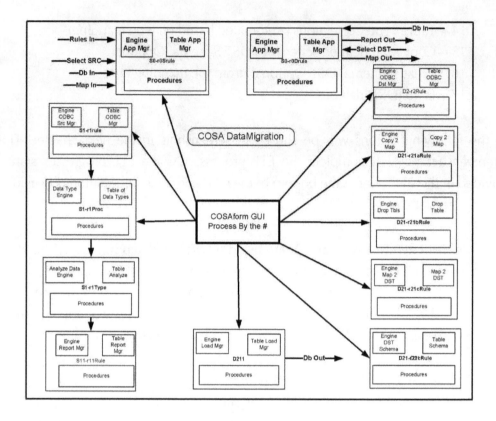

Figure 10.0 – The generalized Data Migration application

The GUI state machine will manage all user interaction and displays progress and information. The GUI design consists of a window in multiple tabs providing various levels of detail about each step of the data migration processes. The first tab shows the source and destination connections. The second tab shows the source, translation, and destination schemas. The third tab shows the quality of the data by allowing the user to query the source connection. The forth tab shows the trace information. The GUI manages the tabs with information being provided by the proper subordinate state machine. Numbered buttons provide chronological shortcut actions to each step in the data migration process.

10.2 – The Initial BNF Specification

ETL and BNF by the Numbers: The easiest way to use the COSA DataMigration application is by the numbers. The first button the user encounters is the zero 'Initialize' button. The instruction in the lower right status bar indicates the current state of the application. The status instruction says, "Click Initialize to Start the COSA-DSPL Service Bus".

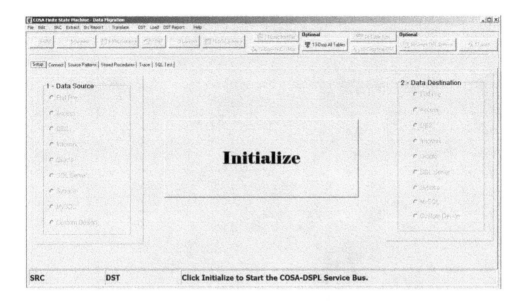

10.1 Step 0 – Initializing the Application

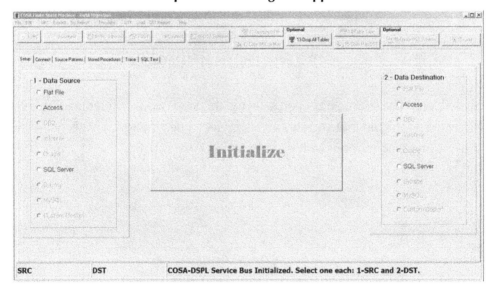

10.2 Step 1 – Select SRC Type

The "Initialize" button has been disabled and the user can now select the Data Source and the Data Destination. The message bar at the bottom of the application displays the SRC and DST connect types when they are selected. The message bar also provides instructions as to what the next action should be. In this example the Data Source types that can be selected are "Flat File", "Access", or "SQL Server" and the Data Destination types that can be selected are "Access" or "SQL Server". Other data connectors can be added to the application. The connection type displays are still showing "SRC" and "DST".

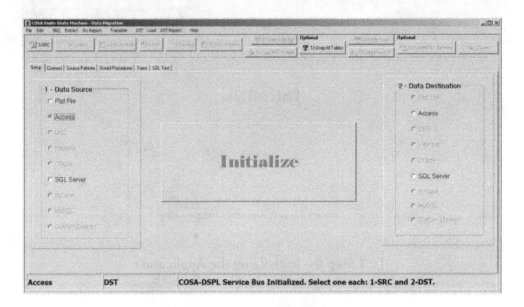

Figure 10.3 Selecting Source Database

Once a first Step data source has been selected the Step two is available to be selected. The instructions indicate that you should also select a destination. That is not necessary if you just want to experiment with examining a source schema.

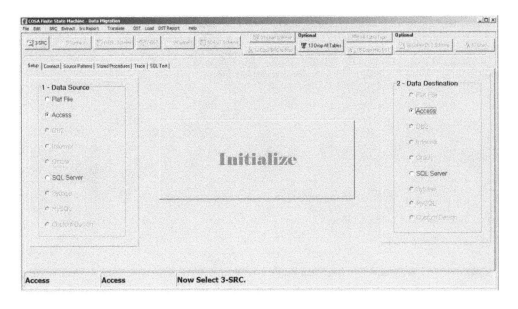

Figure 10.4 Selecting the Access Destination

The source type "Access" has been selected and the status bar has been changed to reflect the type selected.

    S0_Type = SRC;

10.5 Step 2 – Select DST Type

The destination data type has been selected as "Access". This is going to be a simple copy and validate type of operation between two Access databases.

    D0_Type = DST;

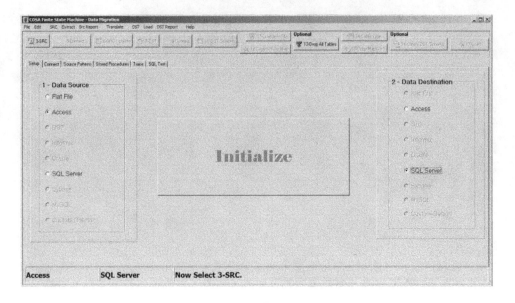

Figure 10.5 Selecting SQL Server Destination

In this example the destination database selected is "SQL Server". This is the example that will be used occasionally throughout this document.

When the Data Source and Data Destination have both been selected the status bar displays both databases type and provides the instruction "Now Select 3-SRC". The "3-SRC" is the first button on the left of the menu bar.

SRC Radio Button Handlers

```
//                                    Next              Next
//             Static     True        True     False    False
// Rules       State      Behavior     Rule     Behavior  Rule      Trace
pS(rType,      isFlatFile, pS0_FlatFile, rType+1, Ignore,  rType+1,  2100);
pS(rType+1,    isAccess,   pS0_Access,   rType+3, Ignore,  rType+2,  2101);
pS(rType+2,    isDB2,      pS0_DB2,      rType+3, Ignore,  rType+3,  2102);
pS(rType+3,    isInformix, pS0_Informix, rType+4, Ignore,  rType+4,  2103);
pS(rType+4,    isOracle,   pS0_Oracle,   rType+5, Ignore,  rType+5,  2104);
pS(rType+5,    isSqlServer,pS0_SQLServer, rType+6, Ignore,  rType+6,  2105);
pS(rType+6,    isSybase,   pS0_Sybase,   rType+7, Ignore,  rType+7,  2106);
pS(rType+7,    isMySql,    pS0_MySQL,    rType+8, Ignore,  rType+8,  2107);
pS(rType+8,    isCustom,   pS0_Custom,   rType+9, Ignore,  rType+9,  2108);

pS(rErr,       iS0_Err,    pS0_Err,      rType,   Ignore,  rType,    2186);
```

DST Radio Button Handlers

```
//                    --                      Next                    Next
//           Static       True               True         False      False
// Rules     State        Behavior           Rule         Behavior   Rule       Trace
pD(rType,    iDFlatFile,  pD0_FlatFile,      rType+1,     Ignore,    rErr,      2150);
pD(rType+1,  iDAccess,    pD0_Access,        rType+2,     Ignore,    rErr,      2151);
pD(rType+2,  iDDB2,       pD0_DB2,           rType+3,     Ignore,    rErr,      2152);
pD(rType+3,  iDInformix,  pD0_Informix,      rType+4,     Ignore,    rErr,      2153);
pD(rType+4,  iDOracle,    pD0_Oracle,        rType+5,     Ignore,    rErr,      2154);
pD(rType+5,  iDSQLServer, pD0_SQLServer,     rType+6,     Ignore,    rErr,      2155);
pD(rType+6,  iDSybase,    pD0_Sybase,        rType+7,     Ignore,    rErr,      2156);
pD(rType+7,  iDMySQL,     pD0_MySQL,         rType+8,     Ignore,    rErr,      2157);
pD(rType+8,  iDCustom,    pD0_Custom,        rType+9,     Ignore,    rErr,      2158);
pD(rErr,     iS0_Err,     pS0_Err,           rType,       Ignore,    rType,     2186);
end:
```

When speed is a consideration this search approach is replaced with vector directly to the type by providing the engine with the "rType+n" value in iTime. For the DST providers the value of each static state is the same as the rule position. The value of iDFlatFile is zero, iDAcess is one, ... , iDMySQL is seven, and iDCustom is eight. All the DST radio button's next false rules jump to the rErr base rule.

Chapter 11

The ETL User Interface

Available SRC Connections:

> S1_SRC = Available Select Connect Extract Disconnect;
> S11_Analyze = TableSelect (Row10 | Row100 | RowAll)
>   OpenDict SaveDict CloseDict;
> S0_Type = SRC DST;

11.1 Step 3 – List Available SRC Databases

The "3-SRC" button uses the ODBC handler to determine what connections are available. The ODBC Administrative tools on Windows create and manages these connections, the SRC connections are in the lower left window.

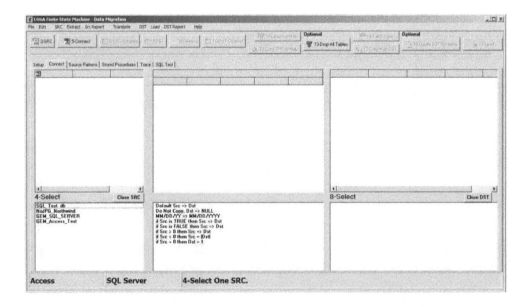

Figure 11.0

After the "3-SRC" button has been selected the available connections are shown in the "4-Select" listbox at the lower left corner of the application. The status bar provides the instruction to "4-Select One SRC". The SRC database type chosen was "Access" so the connection needs to be of the proper type to prevent an error in the connection and translation.

11.2 Step 4 – Select SRC Database

When the Data Source has been selected the chosen element will be highlighted and the name of the connection will be displayed in the status bar. The SRC chosen is "NoJPG_NorthWind".

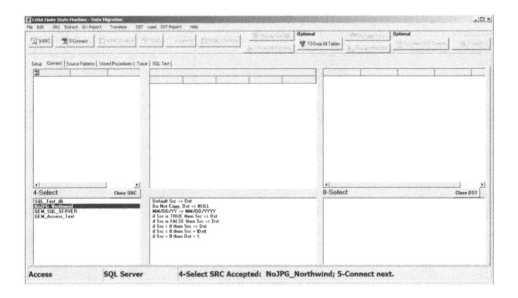

Figure 11.1

In addition, the status bar will provide instructions for the next action "5-Connect next". The "5-Connect" button will be enabled.

11.3 Step 5 – Connect to SRC Database

Clicking on the "5-Connect" button will create an ODBC connection. The status bar will provide the information "Step 5-Source Connected to:" the name of the connection. The connection name will also appear in the left window below the tabs. In addition, the status bar will provide the instruction for the next action "6-SRC Schema next". The window also displays the name of the database connection and highlights the column bar in yellow.

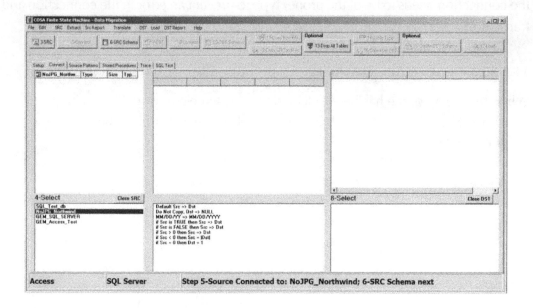

Figure 11.2

The "6-SRC Schema" button will be enabled so the SRC schema can be extracted.

Chapter 12

Access to the Source Schema

Now that we have a connection to a data source the next step is to determine its structure. Even if the connection is to a flat file the ODBC device driver will provide the structure.

12.1 Step 6 – SRC Extract

Clicking on the "6-SRC Schema" will extract the schema and display the structure in the list tree on the left of the application. The tree is expandable and collapsible to provide a compact display of the data source structure.

Now that we have a connection to a data source the next step is to determine its structure. Even if the connection is to a flat file the file will provide the structure as the first line of text.

```
//              Static      True        Next True   False       Next False
//  Rules       State       Behavior    Rule        Behavior    Rule        Trace
p1MCM(rSCnct,   I_S1GETSRC, pS1_GetSRC, rSCnct+1,   Ignore,     rSCnct+1,   3100);
p1MCM(rSCnct+1, I_S1SRCSEL, pS1_Select, rSCnct+2,   Ignore,     rSCnct+2,   3110);
p1MCM(rSCnct+2, I_S1SRCCON, pS1_Conct,  rSCnct+3,   Ignore,     rSCnct+3,   3120);
p1MCM(rSCnct+3, I_S1ChekCn, pS1_EngOff, rExtrt,     pS1_NotGood,rSCnct+1,   3130);

p1MCM(rExtrt,   I_S1SRCEXT, pS1_InitS1, rExtrt+1,   Ignore,     rExtrt+1,   3140);
p1MCM(rExtrt+1, S1_TRUE,    pS1_GetSchma,rExtrt+2,  Ignore,     rExtrt+2,   3150);

p1MCM(rExtrt+2, W_S1TbLtCn, pS1_TblLtCnt,rExtrt+3,  Ignore,     rExtrt+9,   3160);
p1MCM(rExtrt+3, I_Sys,      pS1_SysTbl,  rExtrt+4,  Ignore,     rExtrt+4,   3170);
p1MCM(rExtrt+4, I_View,     pS1_ViewTbl, rExtrt+5,  Ignore,     rExtrt+5,   3180);
p1MCM(rExtrt+5, I_TblUsr,   pS1_TblOrUsr,rExtrt+6,  Ignore,     rExtrt+7,   3190);
p1MCM(rExtrt+6, S1_TRUE,    pS1_Schema,  rExtrt+7,  Ignore,     rExtrt+7,   3200);
p1MCM(rExtrt+7, S1_TRUE,    pS1_NextTbl, rExtrt+8,  Ignore,     rExtrt+8,   3210);
p1MCM(rExtrt+8, S1_TRUE,    pS1_EndTbls, rExtrt+2,  Ignore,     rExtrt+9,   3220);

p1MCM(rExtrt+9, S1_TRUE,    pS1_ClrAll,  rExtrt+10, Ignore,     rExtrt+10,  3230);

p1MCM(rExtrt+10,I_S1ChekCn, pS1_EngOff,  rSCnct,    pS1_NotGood,rErr,       3240);
p1MCM(rExtrt+11,I_S1DisCon, pS1_DisCn,   rSCnct,    Ignore,     rErr,       3250);

p1MCM(rErr,     I_S1Err,    pS1_Err,     rSCnct,    pS1_Err,    rSCnct,     3900);
end;
```

12.0 Source Select-Connect-Extract Table

123

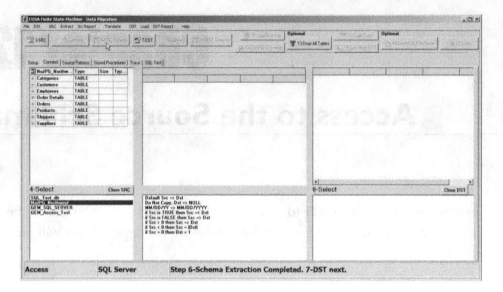

Figure 12.1

Selecting one of the tables and clicking on the "+" will expand the table to display the column information. The columns can be sized if necessary, to show more information. The SRC schema cannot be edited. But if the SRC schema is copied into the map window it can be edited and saved as a new database.

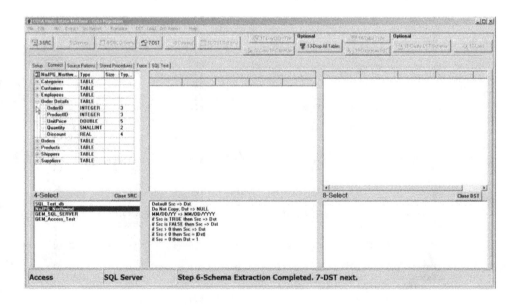

Figure 12.2

Expanding the table to display the column information begins the process of analyzing the data to determine what changes will be required to migrate each column. From experience the "DOUBLE" Access data type does not migrate to SQL Server.

S1_SRC = Available Select Connect Extract Disconnect;
S11_Analyze = TableSelect (Row10 |Row100 |RowAll)
              OpenDict SaveDict CloseDict;
S2_DST = Available Select Connect Extract Drop Create
              Load Commit Disconnect;
S21_Map = SRC2MAP EditMap MAP2DST
        LoadMap SaveMap CloseMap ClearMap;

12.2 The GUI BNF Definition

The GUI only controls the distribution of work to the other more specialized state machine engines. When a listbox or button is clicked the corresponding "OnClick" event calls the proper engine object to begin the action.

GUI OnClick = iGETSRC | iSRCSEL | iSRCCON | iSRCEXT
          | iGETDST | iDSTSEL | iDSTCON | iDSTEXT
          | iSRCCOPY | iDSTDROP | iDSTLOAD
          | iEND | iERR ;

Selecting one of the tables and clicking on the "+" will expand the table to display the column information.

S1_SRC = Available Select Connect Extract Disconnect;
S11_Analyze = TableSelect (Row10 | Row100 | RowAll)
              OpenDict SaveDict CloseDict;
S2_DST = Available Select Connect Extract Drop Create
              Load Commit Disconnect;
S21_Map = SRC2MAP EditMap MAP2DST
        LoadMap SaveMap CloseMap ClearMap;

The extraction includes system level tables.

12.3 GUI On Click BNF Logic

This Temporal table manages the analysis of the source table.

```
//                                    Next                Next
//           Static    True           True      False     False
// Rules     State     Behavior       Rule      Behavior  Rule      Trace
p1Proc(rSProc,  S_GetProcs,  pS1_GetPrcs,   rSProc+1, Ignore,   rSProc+1,  3500);
p1Proc(rSProc+1,S_ClrLst,    pS1_ClrLst,    rSProc+2, Ignore,   rSProc+2,  3510);
p1Proc(rSProc+2,S_SetColHdr, pS1_SetColHdr, rSProc+3, Ignore,   rSProc+3,  3520);
p1Proc(rSProc+3,S_GetPrms,   pS1_GetPrms,   rSProc+4, pS1_NoProcs,rSProc+4,3530);
p1Proc(rSProc+4,S_GetFields, pS1_GetFields, rSProc+5, Ignore,   rSProc+5,  3540);
p1Proc(rSProc+5,I_CntGtZero, pS1_GetPrmTyp, rSProc+6, Ignore,   rSProc+6,  3550);

p1Proc(rSProc+6,I_CntGtZero, pS1_GetPrmTyp, rSProc+7, Ignore,   rSProc+7,  3560);
p1Proc(rSProc+7,I_CntGtZero, pS1_GetPrmTyp, rSProc+8, Ignore,   rSProc+8,  3570);
p1Proc(rSProc+8,I_CntGtZero, pS1_GetPrmTyp, rSProc+9, Ignore,   rSProc+9,  3580);
end;
```

12.3 Get Source Stored Procedures

12.4 Summary

The moving of data from one source to a different destination is very common and happens more often than one would expect. A well-designed set of logic tables makes this a very useful application that can be easily modified to extend the application to cover any data migration strategy.

Chapter 13

Examining the Source Data

SO_Type = SRC DST;
S1_SRC = Available Select Connect Extract Disconnect;

13.1 SRC Data Analysis

A parser engine handles the data analysis.

S11_Analyze = TableSelect (Row10 | Row100 | RowAll)

13.2 Examining the SRC Data

Understanding the data by direct examination is an important part of data migration. The menu "Src Report" allows the user to select any table in the SRC schema and extract data. On the "Source Patterns" tab a list of tables is provided on the right. Clicking on the table name selects the table. Going to the "Src Report" menu then selecting "Display 10 Records" will extract ten records into the spreadsheet at the top of the tab window. The columns are displayed at the top of the spreadsheet with columns that can be sized to view the data.

There are two trees below the spreadsheet that provide data analysis. The left tree provides data structure analysis on the schema. The right tree provides data syntax analysis showing the lexical patterns found in the data.

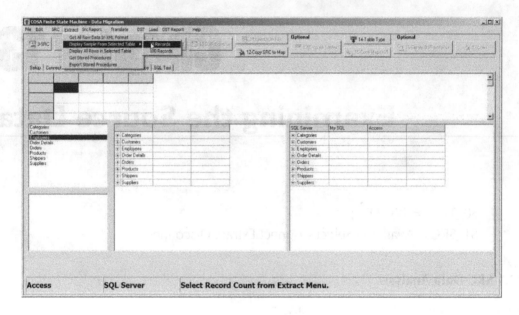

Figure 13.0

13.3 S1 Subordinate Engine

The subordinate engine uses the table to type the data based on the connection type.

```
//                                     Next            Next
//                  Static      True   True    False   False
//      Rules       State       Behavior Rule  Behavior Rule    Trace
plTYPE(rDType,      iGETTYPE,   pColType,  rDType+1,  Ignore,  rDType+1,  3500);
plTYPE(rDType+1,    iGETSize,   pColSize,  rDType+2,  Ignore,  rDType+2,  3505);

plTYPE(rDType+2,    iDB_EMPTY,  pNotAvail, rDType+3,  Ignore,  rDType+3,  3510);
plTYPE(rDType+3,    iDB_NULL,   pNotAvail, rDType+4,  Ignore,  rDType+4,  3515);
plTYPE(rDType+4,    iDB_I2,     pIntgr2,   rDType+5,  Ignore,  rDType+5,  3520);
plTYPE(rDType+5,    iDB_I4,     pIntgr4,   rDType+6,  Ignore,  rDType+6,  3525);
plTYPE(rDType+6,    iDB_R4,     pDbl4,     rDType+7,  Ignore,  rDType+7,  3530);
plTYPE(rDType+7,    iDB_R8,     pDbl8,     rDType+8,  Ignore,  rDType+8,  3535);
plTYPE(rDType+8,    iDB_CY,     pNotAvail, rDType+9,  Ignore,  rDType+9,  3540);
plTYPE(rDType+9,    iDB_DATE,   pDate,     rDType+10, Ignore,  rDType+10, 3545);
plTYPE(rDType+10,   iDB_BSTR,   pText,     rDType+11, Ignore,  rDType+11, 3550);
plTYPE(rDType+11,   iDB_IDISPATCH,pNotAvail, rDType+12, Ignore, rDType+12, 3555);

plTYPE(rDType+12,   iDB_ERROR,  pNotAvail, rDType+13, Ignore,  rDType+13, 3560);

plTYPE(rDType+13,   iDB_BOOL,   pBit,      rDType+14, Ignore,  rDType+14, 3565);
plTYPE(rDType+14,   iDB_NUMERIC, pNumeric, rDType+15, Ignore,  rDType+15, 3568);
plTYPE(rDType+15,   iDB_VARIANT, pText,    rDType+16, Ignore,  rDType+16, 3570);
plTYPE(rDType+16,   iDB_IUNKNOWN, pNotAvail, rDType+17, Ignore, rDType+17, 3575);
plTYPE(rDType+17,   iDB_DECIMAL, pDecimal, rDType+18, Ignore,  rDType+18, 3580);
plTYPE(rDType+18,   iDB_BYTES,  pByte,     rDType+19, Ignore,  rDType+19, 3585);
plTYPE(rDType+19,   iDB_STR,    pText,     rDType+20, Ignore,  rDType+20, 3590);
plTYPE(rDType+20,   iDB_WSTR,   pMemo,     rDType+21, Ignore,  rDType+21, 3595);
plTYPE(rDType+21,   iDB_DBTIMESTAMP,pDate, rDType+22, Ignore,  rDType+22, 3615);
plTYPE(rNotAvail,   0,          pNotAvail, rDType,    pNotAvail,rDType,   3625);
```

13.1 Analyzing Source Data Types

When the source data is being analyzed there are a number of features that can be used to get a well-defined picture of the elements of the data.

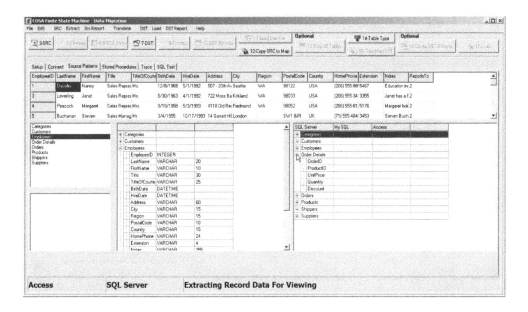

Figure 13.2

```
//            Static    True         Next True    False        Next False
//    Rules   State     Behavior     Rule         Behavior     Rule        Trace
pllMCM(rAlz,    I_TblSel,  pSll_TblSel,  rAlz+1,  Ignore,      rAlz+1,    4100);
pllMCM(rAlz+1,  I_Select,  pSll_Table,   rAlz+2,  pSll_NoTable, rDone,    4110);
pllMCM(rAlz+2,  I_Row10,   pSll_Row10,   rAlz+3,  Ignore,      rAlz+3,    4120);
pllMCM(rAlz+3,  I_Row100,  pSll_Row100,  rAlz+4,  Ignore,      rAlz+4,    4130);
pllMCM(rAlz+4,  I_RowAll,  pSll_RowAll,  rAlz+5,  Ignore,      rAlz+5,    4140);
pllMCM(rAlz+5,  I_SelTN,   pSll_ExtRows, rAlz+6,  pSll_NotSeld, rDone,    4150);
pllMCM(rAlz+6,  I_OpenD,   pSll_OpenDct, rAlz+7,  Ignore,      rAlz+7,    4160);
pllMCM(rAlz+7,  I_SaveD,   pSll_SaveDct, rAlz+8,  Ignore,      rAlz+8,    4170);
pllMCM(rAlz+8,  I_ClosD,   pSll_ClsDct,  rAlz+9,  Ignore,      rAlz+9,    4180);
pllMCM(rAlz+9,  I_Analz,   pSll_Analyze, rAlz+10, Ignore,      rAlz+10,   4190);
pllMCM(rAlz+10, I_Repar,   pSll_Repair,  rAlz+11, Ignore,      rAlz+11,   4200);

pllMCM(rDone,   I_Sll_Err, pSll_Err,     rAlz,    Ignore,      rAlz,      4976);
pllMCM(rErr,    I_Sll_Err, pSll_Err,     rAlz,    Ignore,      rAlz,      4986);
```

13.3 Allow User to Display Source Data

13.4 SRC More Detailed Analysis

Figure 13.4 shows two StringGrids. The top grid is the data and the bottom grid is the data pattern expressed as a regular expression. An immediate flag can be seen in the

Postal Code column. The regular expression is '9+', then there comes the '**A+9[WS]9A+**', this pattern is caused by the 'WA1 1DP' postal code from the UK.

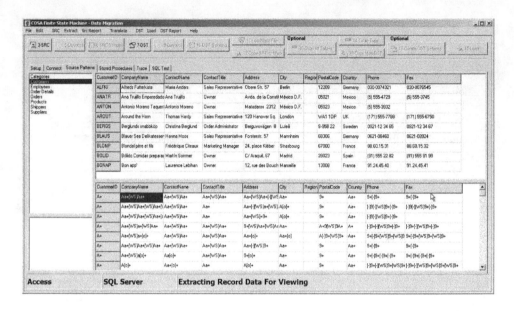

Figure 13.4 – Examining the Data

13.5 SRC Extract All Rows

The menu under "Extract" allows the user to examine the data. The "Source Patterns" tab analysis includes the detailed structure of the data displayed in BNF notation. This provides the data steward or analyst with the detail to plan for what to expect in the data structure. Knowing the data structure and its anomalies might help recognize where corruption might occur, and how to best use the data.

S2_DST = Available Select Connect Extract Drop Create
            Load Commit Disconnect;
S21_Map = SRC2MAP EditMap MAP2DST
        LoadMap SaveMap CloseMap ClearMap;

Analysis in this example shows the Employee record schema, examine the typing for each of the table's elements.

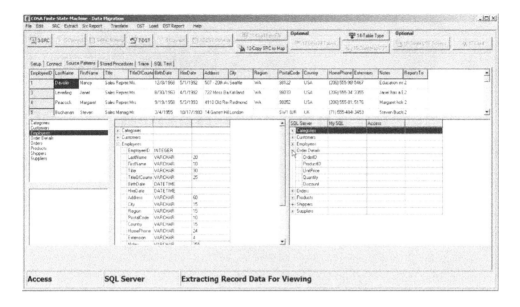

Figure 13.5

13.6 S11 Extract Data Logic

```
//              Static    True                  Next True    False          Next False
//     Rules    State     Behavior              Rule         Behavior       Rule         Trace
p11MCM(rAlz,    I_TblSel, pS11_TblSel,  rAlz+1,  Ignore,      rAlz+1,   4100);
p11MCM(rAlz+1,  I_Select, pS11_Table,   rAlz+2,  pS11_NoTable, rDone,   4110);
p11MCM(rAlz+2,  I_Row10,  pS11_Row10,   rAlz+3,  Ignore,      rAlz+3,   4120);
p11MCM(rAlz+3,  I_Row100, pS11_Row100,  rAlz+4,  Ignore,      rAlz+4,   4130);
p11MCM(rAlz+4,  I_RowAll, pS11_RowAll,  rAlz+5,  Ignore,      rAlz+5,   4140);
p11MCM(rAlz+5,  I_SelTN,  pS11_ExtRows, rAlz+6,  pS11_NotSeld, rDone,   4150);
p11MCM(rAlz+6,  I_OpenD,  pS11_OpenDct, rAlz+7,  Ignore,      rAlz+7,   4160);
p11MCM(rAlz+7,  I_SaveD,  pS11_SaveDct, rAlz+8,  Ignore,      rAlz+8,   4170);
p11MCM(rAlz+8,  I_ClosD,  pS11_ClsDct,  rAlz+9,  Ignore,      rAlz+9,   4190);
p11MCM(rAlz+9,  I_Analz,  pS11_Analyze, rAlz+10, Ignore,      rAlz+10,  4190);
p11MCM(rAlz+10, I_Repar,  pS11_Repair,  rAlz+11, Ignore,      rAlz+11,  4200);

p11MCM(rDone,   I_S11_Err, pS11_Err,    rAlz,    Ignore,      rAlz,     4976);
p11MCM(rErr,    I_S11_Err, pS11_Err,    rAlz,    Ignore,      rAlz,     4986);
```

13.6 Allow user to display data, 10, 100 or all rows in selected table

Chapter 14

Accessing the Destination Schema

SRC and DST Schemas Extracted

Make sure that the system was properly backed up and that a test copy is being used until every aspect of the ETL process has been verified. Be safe and be smart when using this ETL process. The data you might destroy might by your own.

S0_Type = SRC DST;
S1_SRC = Available Select Connect Extract Disconnect;
S11_Analyze = TableSelect (Row10 | Row100 | RowAll)
        OpenDict SaveDict CloseDict;

14.1 Available DST Connections

S2_DST = Available Select Connect Extract Drop Create
        Load Commit Disconnect;
S21_Map = SRC2MAP EditMap MAP2DST LoadMap

SaveMap CloseMap ClearMap;

14.2 Step 7 – View Available DST Databases

The "7-DST" button uses the ODBC handler to determine what connections are available. The ODBC Administrative tools on Windows create and manages these connections. The available connections are displayed in the lower right window.

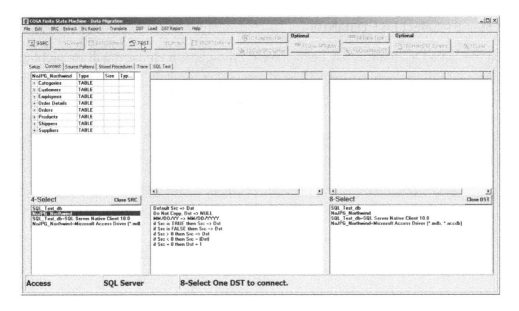

Figure 14.0

D2 Logic

```
//              Static       True          Next True   False        Next False
//   Rules      State        Behavior      Rule        Behavior     Rule          Trace
pMCM(rDCnct,    I_GETDST,    pD2_GetDST,   rDCnct+1,   Ignore,      rDCnct+1,     5100);
pMCM(rDCnct+1,  I_DSTSEL,    pD2_Select,   rDCnct+2,   Ignore,      rDCnct+2,     5110);
pMCM(rDCnct+2,  I_DSTCON,    pD2_Connect,  rDExt,      Ignore,      rDCnct+3,     5120);

pMCM(rDExt,     I_DSTEXT,    pD2_Extrct,   rDExt+1,    pD2_NoDST,   rDCnct,       5130);
pMCM(rDExt+1,   I_TRUE,      pD2_GetSchma, rDExt+2,    Ignore,      rDExt+1,      5140);

pMCM(rDExt+2,   W_TblLtCnt,  pD2_TblLtCnt, rDExt+3,    Ignore,      rDExt+3,      5150);
pMCM(rDExt+3,   I_SysTbl,    pD2_SysTbl,   rDExt+7,    Ignore,      rDExt+4,      5160);
pMCM(rDExt+4,   I_ViewTbl,   pD2_ViewTbl,  rDExt+7,    Ignore,      rDExt+5,      5170);
pMCM(rDExt+5,   I_TblUser,   pD2_TblOrUsr, rDExt+6,    Ignore,      rDExt+7,      5180);
pMCM(rDExt+6,   I_TRUE,      pD2_Schema,   rDExt+7,    Ignore,      rDExt+7,      5190);
pMCM(rDExt+7,   I_TRUE,      pD2_NextTbl,  rDExt+2,    Ignore,      rDExt+8,      5200);

pMCM(rDExt+8,   I_TRUE,      pD2_EndTbls,  rDExt+9,    Ignore,      rDExt+9,      5010);
pMCM(rDExt+9,   I_TRUE,      pD2_EngOff,   rDExt+10,   Ignore,      rDExt+10,     5200);

pMCM(rErr,      I_Error,     pD2_Error,    rDCnct,     pD2_Error,   rDCnct,       5916);
```

14.1 Connect to Destination – Extract Schema

14.3 Step 8 – Select DST Database

When the Data Destination has been selected the chosen element will be highlighted and the name of the connection will be displayed in the light blue status bar in Figure 14.3.

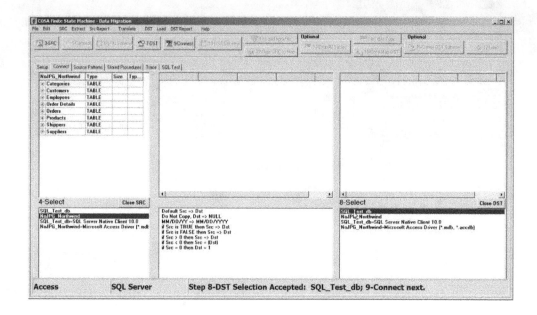

Figure 14.2

S2_DST = Available Select Connect Extract Drop Create
     Load Commit Disconnect;
S21_Map = SRC2MAP EditMap MAP2DST
LoadMap SaveMap CloseMap ClearMap;

14.4 Step 9 – Connect to DST Database

Clicking on the "9-Connect" button will create an ODBC connection. The status bar will provide the information "Step 9-DST Connected to:" the name of the connection. The connection name will also appear in the RIGHT window below the tabs. In addition, the status bar will provide the instruction for the next action "10-DST Schema next".

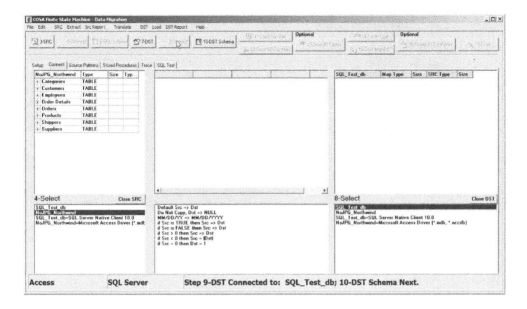

Figure 14.3

The "10-DST Schema" button will be enabled allowing the schema to be extracted and displayed as in Figure 14.3 under the status line.

14.5 Step 10 – Extracting the Destination Schema

Now that we have a connection to a data destination the next step is to determine its structure. Even if the connection is to a flat file the ODBC device driver will provide the structure. If the structure is a blank test destination the structure will be empty.

S0_Type = SRC DST;
S1_SRC = Available Select Connect Extract Disconnect;
S11_Analyze = TableSelect (Row10 | Row100 | RowAll)
          OpenDict SaveDict CloseDict;

Clicking on the "10-DST Schema" will extract the schema and display the structure in the list tree on the RIGHT of the application. The tree is expandable and collapsible to provide a compact display of the data destination structure.

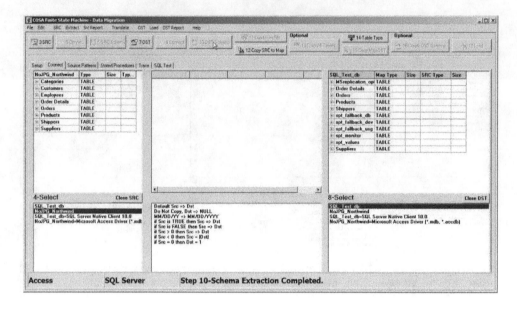

Figure 14.4

DST Schema Extraction

S2_DST = Available Select Connect Extract Drop Create
     Load Commit Disconnect;
S21_Map = SRC2MAP EditMap MAP2DST LoadMap
     SaveMap CloseMap ClearMap;

14.6 Step 11 – Load Schema from File

Not implemented at this time

Chapter 15
The Mapping State Machine

S0_Type = SRC DST;

S1_SRC = Available Select Connect Extract Disconnect;

S11_Analyze = TableSelect (Row10 | Row100 | RowAll)
        OpenDict SaveDict CloseDict;

S2_DST = Available Select Connect Extract Drop Create
        Load Commit Disconnect;

Using the SRC Schema

S21_Map = SRC2MAP EditMap MAP2DST

15.1 Step 12 – Copy SRC to MAP

Step 12 directly copies the source map into the mapping area in the center display tree. The mapping tree can be examined and edited. Clicking on the plus sign for each table will display the columns.

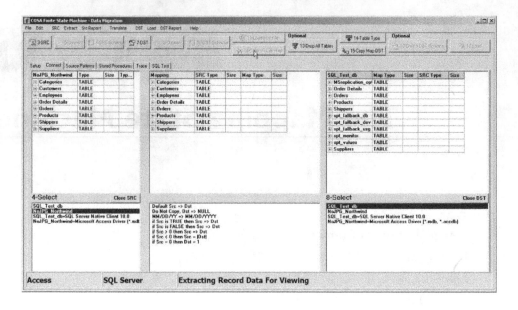

Figure 15.0

D21 Mapping Logic

```
//                                    Next            Next
//             Static     True        True    False   False
//    Rules    State      Behavior     Rule    Behavior  Rule      Trace
pMCM(rMap,    iLoadMAP,  pD21_LoadMap, rMap+1, Ignore,  rMap+1,   6100);
pMCM(rMap+1,  iSRCCOPY,  pD21_SRC2MAP, rMap+2, Ignore,  rMap+2,   6110);
pMCM(rMap+2,  iEditMap,  pD21_EditMap, rMap+3, Ignore,  rMap+3,   6120);
pMCM(rMap+3,  iSaveMAP,  pD21_SaveMap, rMap+4, Ignore,  rMap+4,   6130);
pMCM(rMap+4,  iDSTDROP,  pD21_DropDST, rMap+5, Ignore,  rMap+5,   6140);
pMCM(rMap+5,  iMAP2DST,  pD21_MAP2DST, rMap+6, Ignore,  rMap+6,   6150);
pMCM(rMap+6,  iCRSCHMA,  pD21_CrSchma, rMap+7, Ignore,  rErr,     6160);

pMCM(rErr,    iD21_Err,  pD21_Err,     rMap,   Ignore,  rMap,     6986);
```

15.1 Manage Mapping and Destination Schema

15.2 Modifying the SRC Schema

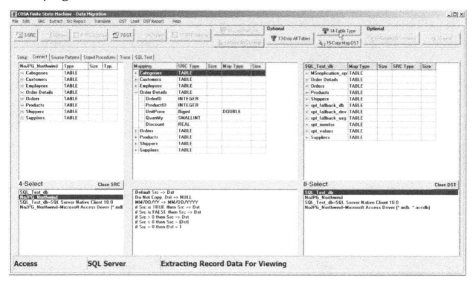

Figure 15.2

15.3 Saving the New Schema

Map = LoadMap | CopySrc2Map | SaveMap | Drop Dst

 Map2Dst | CreateDstSchema;

Dropping the DST Schema will cause all the data to be lost. Be very careful when using 13-Drop All Tables. NOTE: Drop All Tables does not drop the SRC Tables. It is possible to drop the source table if the source table is connected as a destination source. Be careful when connecting to the destination source.

```
//                                  Next            Next
//              Static    True       True      False     False
//    Rules     State     Behavior   Rule      Behavior  Rule       Trace
pMCM(rMap,      iLoadMAP, pD21_LoadMap, rMap+1,  Ignore,   rMap+1,    8100);
pMCM(rMap+1,    iSRCCOPY, pD21_SRC2MAP, rMap+2,  Ignore,   rMap+2,    8110);
pMCM(rMap+2,    iEditMap, pD21_EditMap, rMap+3,  Ignore,   rMap+3,    8120);
pMCM(rMap+3,    iSaveMAP, pD21_SaveMap, rMap+4,  Ignore,   rMap+4,    8130);
pMCM(rMap+4,    iDSTDROP, pD21_DropDST, rMap+5,  Ignore,   rMap+5,    8140);
pMCM(rMap+5,    iMAP2DST, pD21_MAP2DST, rMap+6,  Ignore,   rMap+6,    8150);
pMCM(rMap+6,    iCRSCHMA, pD21_CrSchma, rMap+7,  Ignore,   rErr,      8160);

pMCM(rErr,      iD21_Err, pD21_Err,    rMap,    Ignore,   rMap,      8900);
```

Figure 15.3

15.4 Step 13 – Drop All Tables

When the DST schema has been compromised or when there is sufficient reason to drop the DST schema for a fresh start; then use the OPTIONAL 13-Drop Tables button.

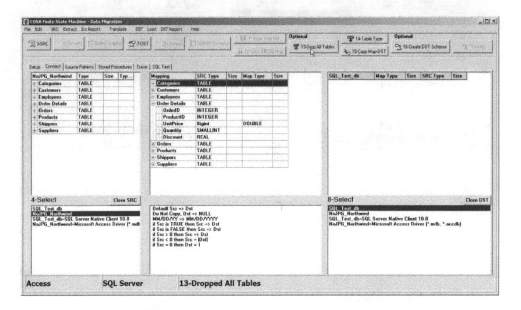

Figure 15.4

After the DST Schema has been dropped it can be created by copying the Mapped Schema into the destination using button 15-Copy Map DST. The other option is to edit the DST schema display directly, create all the tables, and their data type.

15.5 Step 14 – Table Type fixing the SRC to DST data type

It would be nice if there were one standard data type amongst all databases. Sadly, it is not so. Therefore, each table must be analyzed to determine if the columns will map from the SRC to the DST.

15.6 Step 15 – Copy Map to DST

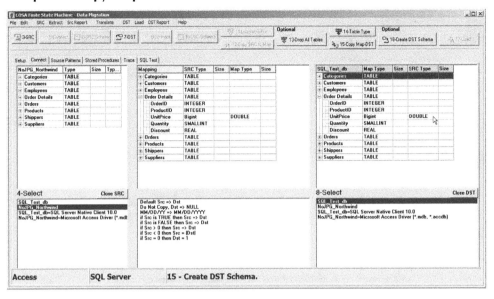

Figure 15.5 Mapping SRC onto and into DST

```
//                              Next            Next
//          Static    True      True    False   False
//   Rules  State     Behavior  Rule    Behavior Rule    Trace
pBJb(rCRS,  I_DSTcon, piD21_DSTCon,  rCRS+1,  pD21_EngOff,rCRS,  6100);
pBJb(rCRS+1, W_TblLTCnt, pwD21_TblLTCnt, rCRS+2, pD21_EngOff,rCRS+2, 6110);
pBJb(rCRS+2, I_UnqTbl,  piD21_UnqTbl,  rCRS+3,  Ignore,  rCRS+3,  6115);
pBJb(rCRS+3, I_TblOrUsr, piD21_TblOrUsr, rCRS+4, Ignore,  rCRS+14, 6125);
pBJb(rCRS+4, W_ColLTCnt, pwD21_ColLTCnt, rCRS+5, Ignore,  rCRS+13, 6131);
pBJb(rCRS+5, I_UnqCol,  piD21_UnqCol,  rCRS+6,  Ignore,  rCRS+11, 6135);
pBJb(rCRS+6, I_ColTyp,  piD21_ColTyp,  rCRS+7,  Ignore,  rCRS+7,  6140);
pBJb(rCRS+7, E_Node3and4, peD21_Node3and4, rCRS+8, Ignore, rCRS+8, 6145);

pBJb(rCRS+8, I_Flatfile, piD21_FlatFile, rCRS+11, Ignore, rCRS+9, 6150);
pBJb(rCRS+9, I_Access,  piD21_Access,  rCRS+11, Ignore,  rCRS+10, 6155);
pBJb(rCRS+10, I_SQLSvr, piD21_SQLServer, rCRS+11, Ignore, rCRS+11, 6160);

pBJb(rCRS+11, E_UnqCol,  peD21_UnqCol,  rCRS+12, Ignore,  rCRS+12, 6165);
pBJb(rCRS+12, S_IncColNum, psD21_IncColNum, rCRS+13, Ignore, rCRS+13, 6170);
pBJb(rCRS+13, E_ColLTCnt, peD21_ColLtCnt, rCRS+4, Ignore, rCRS+14, 6175);
pBJb(rCRS+14, E_TblType, peD21_TblType, rCRS+15, Ignore, rCRS+15, 6180);
pBJb(rCRS+15, S_IncTblNum, psD21_IncTblNum, rCRS+16, Ignore, rCRS+16, 6185);
pBJb(rCRS+16, E_TblLTcnt, Ignore,       rCRS+1,  peD21_TblLtCnT,rCRS, 6190);
```

15.6 Create Schemas for Each Table

15.7 Step 16 – Create DST Schema

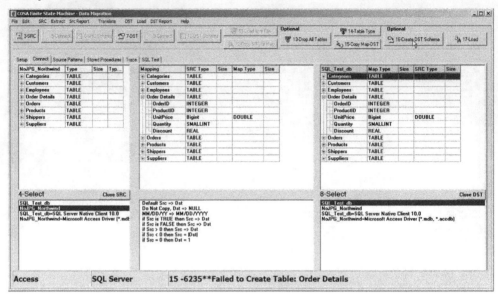

Figure 15.7

D21 Create DST Schema Logic

```
// Create Table Section
//                                    Next              Next
//            Static      True        True    False     False
//  Rules     State       Behavior    Rule    Behavior  Rule      Trace
pBJc(rCRS+0, B_TRUE,      pbD21_InitCrtTbl,rCRS+1, Ignore,   rDone,    6200);
pBJc(rCRS+1, W_TblLtCnt,  pwD21_CrTblLtCnt,rCRS+2, Ignore,   rDone,    6205);
pBJc(rCRS+2, W_ColLtCnt,  pwD21_CrColLtCnt,rCRS+3, Ignore,   rCRS+6,   6215);
pBJc(rCRS+3, I_SzGTZero,  piD21_SizeGtZero,rCRS+4, piD21_SizeLtZero,rCRS+4,6220);

pBJc(rCRS+4, I_ColLtCml,  piD21_ColLtCml,  rCRS+5, plD21_ColLtCml,rCRS+6, 6225);
pBJc(rCRS+5, E_IncColNum, peD21_IncColNum, rCRS+2, Ignore,   rCRS+2,   6230);
pBJc(rCRS+6, B_TRUE,      pbD21_CrtTbl,    rCRS+7, Ignore,   rCRS+7,   6235);
pBJc(rCRS+7, S_IncTblNum, peD21_IncTblNum, rCRS+8, Ignore,   rCRS+8,   6240);
pBJc(rCRS+8, E_TblLtCnt,  Ignore,          rCRS+1, peD21_TblLtCnT,rDone, 6245);

pBJc(rDone,  B_TRUE,      peD21_DONE,      rCRS,   peD21_DONE, rCRS,   6299);
pBJc(rERR,   B_TRUE,      peD21_ERROR,     rCRS,   peD21_ERROR,rCRS,   6296);
...
```

15.8 Create Tables from Schemas

Chapter 16

Extracting, Translating, and Loading

Now the work begins...getting the SQL Server to accept Access data types

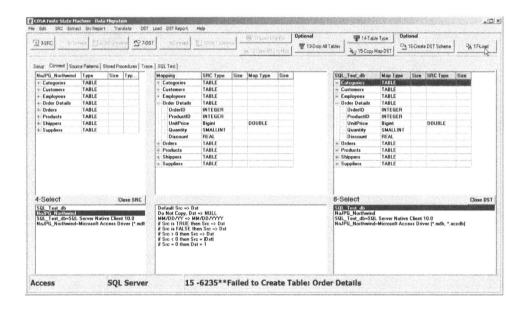

Figure 16.0 – Extracting, Translating, and Loading

16.1 Step 17 – Loading Data

The loading data VSM and logic checks the SRC and DST connections. If either connection is missing the VSM reports the missing connection and stops the VSM.

With the proper connections the various counters are cleared, and the table count is taken from the DST tree structure. The connections strings as re-established. The table number is compared to the table count as the top of the load table loop. If the check table count is true, the DST table name and DST table type is taken from the DST tree. If the table type is 'TABLE' or 'USER' then the table counter is incremented.

In a while loop the DST column name and the column 'type' are placed in string array for this current table. The column names are placed in a string separated by commas to be used in an upcoming SQL statement. Using the DST names could create a problem if the SRC names do not exist. There needs to be a check added to the logic.

SQL 'select' column names 'from' table name statement is built. The 'execute' is contained in a 'try' / 'except' error handler. If an error happens the command and connection are saved in a 'SQL_Load_D211' error log. Regardless of what happens the record counter is set to 1;

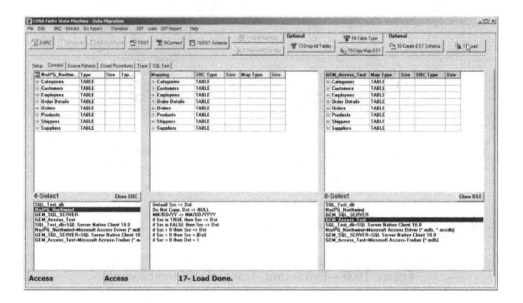

Figure 16.1

The ETL Access to SQL Server is trying to insert an Access Integer into a SQL Server BigInt.

The schema for the SQL Server did not support the Access data types. I switched everything to Integer to get the data to load and left it at that for now. Just changing the map data type did not work. One of the features I will add includes data type mapping when loading from one database type to a different database type.

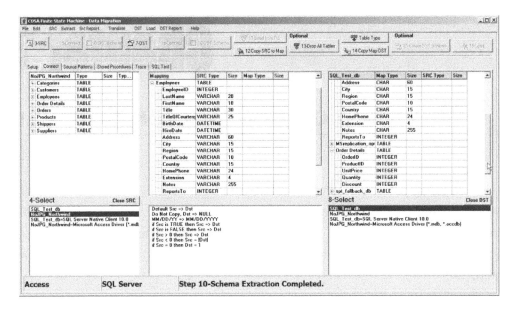

Figure 16.2

```
//                         True          Next                    Next
//                         True          True      False         False
//    Rules     State      Behavior      Rule      Behavior      Rule        Trace
pBJ(rLoad,    I_SRCcon,   pD211_Ignore,   rLoad+1, pD211_NoSRC,  rLoad+1,   7100);
pBJ(rLoad+1,  I_DSTcon,   pD211_Ignore,   rLoad+2, pD211_NoDST,  rLoad+2,   7110);
pBJ(rLoad+2,  S_Init,     pD211_Ignore,   rLoad+3, pD211_Ignore, rLoad+3,   7120);
pBJ(rLoad+3,  I_TblLtCnt, pD211_BuildTbls, rLoad+4, pD211_Ignore, rLoad+4,   7130);
pBJ(rLoad+4,  I_TblOrUsr, pD211_IncTblNum, rLoad+5, pD211_Else_ITN, rLoad+5, 7140);
pBJ(rLoad+5,  W_ColLtCnt, pD211_ColLtCnt,  rLoad+6, pD211_Ignore, rLoad+6,   7150);
pBJ(rLoad+6,  S_TRUE,     pD211_SQLselect, rLoad+7, pD211_Ignore, rLoad+7,   7160);
pBJ(rLoad+7,  W_NotEOF,   pD211_SQLinsert1, rLoad+8, pD211_Ignore, rLoad+8,  7170);
pBJ(rLoad+8,  W_ColLtNum, pD211_SQLinsert2, rLoad+9, pD211_Ignore, rLoad+9,  7180);
pBJ(rLoad+9,  I_LenZero,  pD211_NullError, rLoad+10, pD211_Ignore, rLoad+10, 7190);

pBJ(rLoad+10, S_TRUE,     pD211_BuildColl, rLoad+11, pD211_Ignore, rLoad+11, 7200);
pBJ(rLoad+11, I_ColLtCntM1, pD211_BuildCol2, rLoad+12, pD211_Ignore, rLoad+12, 7210);
pBJ(rLoad+12, S_TRUE,     pD211_IncColNum, rLoad+13, pD211_Ignore, rLoad+13, 7220);
pBJ(rLoad+13, I_DstNotNil, pD211_NxtDstCol, rLoad+14, pD211_Ignore, rLoad+14, 7230);

pBJ(rLoad+14, I_PtnNotNil, pD211_NxtPtnCol, rLoad+15, pD211_Ignore, rLoad+15, 7240);
pBJ(rLoad+15, S_TRUE,     pD211_TryExecSQL, rLoad+16, pD211_Ignore, rLoad+16, 7250);
pBJ(rLoad+16, S_TRUE,     peD211_NotEof,   rLoad+17, pD211_Ignore, rLoad+17, 7260);
pBJ(rLoad+17, S_TRUE,     peD211_Table,    rLoad+18, pD211_Ignore, rLoad+18, 7270);
pBJ(rLoad+18, S_TRUE,     peD211_Conctd,   rLoad+19, pD211_Ignore, rLoad+19, 7280);
pBJ(rLoad+19, S_TRUE,     peD211_ADOsrc,   rLoad+20, pD211_Ignore, rLoad+20, 7290);
pBJ(rErr,     S_Init,     pD211_Error,     rLoad,   pD211_Ignore, rLoad+1,   7900);
```

16.3 Extract Translate Load

Chapter 17

Moving Toward Better Software

There is a better way to produce software, but it takes getting past a lot of cultural barriers, the not invented here, the risk adverseness, and the tendency to take only evolutionary steps. To the senior engineer and managers here are six things I recommend:

1) Use BNF to define everything. Everything you do will eventually become a well-defined BNF BECAUES THAT IS WHAT COMPILERS DO.
2) Expect time to be defined everywhere; even asynchronous events have a well-defined temporal component BECAUSE THAT IS WHAT COMPILERS DO.
3) Follow the COSA paradigm for temporal engineering; spatial programming does not work, recognize it, and avoid it.
4) Do not succumb to the dark side of ITE, it leads to spatial programming. You can find the temporal logic using COSA that will make it work.
5) Demand the support you need to stay synchronized from the specification to testing; everyone wins with better quality reusable software.
6) It takes an engineering discipline. Avoid the shortcuts. Understand the logic. Just say no to ITE.

There are significant benefits moving from an ad hoc approach to creating software to a very structured paradigm like COSA. With the COSA paradigm an industry will develop providing tools that will analyze the logic and the data manipulation in great detail. These tools will include multi-threaded analysis because COSA uses an orthogonal architecture. This analysis will have a much better understanding of the parallel threaded logic.

17.1 The Fundamentals

When the fundamentals of software development are as ad hoc as they currently are the industry has a problem. When software engineering is about the management of document control there are not any fundamentals. With those two sentences I have probably stepped on a lot of toes, but I believe there have been many valid attempts to produce better software through standards, reuse, patterns, object tools, data tools, and many other ideas. As multi-core technology becomes the dominant processor technology and multi-threading becomes the way of getting more throughput, the core software development technology becomes even more important. The problem is that there are not any core development technologies or paradigms. The good news is that COSA provides a core paradigm that can create significantly better-quality software. Provided that the tenants of the COSA paradigm are not violated. The quality of the software being produced by companies using this new paradigm will begin to improve.

17.2 Summary

It is going to take a significant amount of effort to turn the battleship paradigm that is currently the ITE approach to software development. All the new 'agile' paradigms will not fix the fundamental problem.

Epilogue

A well-formed communication is simple and elegant. The description of that communication can be diagrammed in BNF. The rules that make up business, engineering, science, government, law, or military tactics can be collected in a multitude of simple BNF definitions. These definitions become like the secret formula for Coke® well understood and guarded.

A significant amount of ambiguity can be removed from logic using a COSA Extended BNF approach. The task of moving billions of lines of spaghetti code into a COSA framework is not as daunting as it might seem, but it will never happen without a commitment to change at all levels.

The greatest challenge to better software is that people are very resistant to change[46]. People need to see a very gradual evolution in technology. Because this need for a gradual change is true, individuals and groups become a part of the "reluctance to change[47]" syndrome. History is full of stories about reluctance to change: the revolutionary concepts of germs, the sun at the center of the solar system, the copy machine, the automobile, computers, and many more. But once the change starts it will grow like wildfire.

As a taxpayer I would certainly like to see the software used by the government improved. Imagine what NSA, DARPA, NASA, NOAA, and the IRS could do with this technological improvement. The clandestine agencies should be open to investigate any improvements in software. All these institutions should embrace change, especially if there is a significant chance an improvement will result.

Jiri Soukup the author of "The Inevitable Cycle: Graphical Tools and Programming Paradigms", *IEEE Computer*, August 2007, wrote; "Each time the idea of designing software with graphical tools becomes popular, a transition to a new, more powerful programming paradigm makes these tools obsolete. If this observation is correct, the

---

[46] Ernst von Glaserfeld, "The Reluctance to Change a Way of Thinking*", Irish Journal of Psychology, 1988.
[47] Linda Tucci, "Fear factor puts big chill on IT projects", 09 June 2005, SearchCIO.com, http://www.strysik.com/Lead_315_Reluctance_to_Change.html

Unified Modeling Language's current popularity indicates we're approaching the next major paradigm shift." Time will tell.

Lesson Learned

I have included on the next page the poem "The Calf Path" by Sam Walter Foss because I believe this is a good metaphor of how ITE software got started and why it still exists today. This poem certainly addresses the "reluctance to change."

The Calf Path

Sam Walter Foss (1858-1911)

One day through the primeval wood
A calf walked home as good calves should;
But made a trail all bent askew,
A crooked trail as all calves do.
Since then three hundred years have fled,
And I infer the calf is dead.

But still he left behind his trail,
And thereby hangs my moral tale.
The trail was taken up next day
By a lone dog that passed that way;
And then a wise bell-wether sheep
Pursued the trail o'er vale and steep,
And drew the flock behind him, too,
As good bell-wethers always do.

And from that day, o'er hill and glade,
Through those old woods a path was made,
And many men wound in and out,
And dodged and turned and bent about,
And uttered words of righteous wrath
Because 'twas such a crooked path;

But still they followed-do not laugh-
The first migrations of that calf,
And through this winding wood-way stalked
Because he wobbled when he walked.

This forest path became a lane,
That bent, and turned, and turned again.
This crooked lane became a road,
Where many a poor horse with his load
Toiled on beneath the burning sun,
And traveled some three miles in one.

And thus a century and a half
They trod the footsteps of that calf.
The years passed on in swiftness fleet.

The road became a village street;
And this, before men were aware,
A city's crowded thoroughfare,
And soon the central street was this
Of a renowned metropolis;
And men two centuries and a half
Trod in the footsteps of that calf.

Each day a hundred thousand rout
Followed this zigzag calf about,
And o'er his crooked journey went
The traffic of a continent.
A hundred thousand men were led
By one calf near three centuries dead.

They followed still his crooked way,
And lost one hundred years a day,
For thus such reverence is lent
To well-established precedent.
A moral lesson this might teach
Were I ordained and called to preach;

For men are prone to go it blind
Along the calf-paths of the mind,
And work away from sun to sun
To do what other men have done.
They follow in the beaten track,
And out and in, and forth and back,
And still their devious course pursue,
To keep the path that others do.

They keep the path a sacred groove,
Along which all their lives they move;
But how the wise old wood-gods laugh,
Who saw the first primeval calf.
Ah, many things this tale might teach-
But I am not ordained to preach.

Appendix A – COSA Trace File

Static and Dynamic States: Add = 43; Sub = 44; Mul = 42; Div = 47;
                               Digit = 1; Negate = 44; Period = 59;

Date= 12/17/2018
Start of Calculator Trace File.

Time	True/False,	Dynamic,	Trace,	Result
T= 01;	B= fNeg44,	Negate,	100 ;	N= -
T= 02;	B= fDigit,	Any_Number,	101 ;	N= -3
T= 03;	-B= fDigit,	Any_Number,	101 ;	N= -3
T= 04;	B= fDot59,	One_Period,	102 ;	N= -3.
T= 05;	B= fDigit,	Any_Number,	103 ;	N= -3.1
T= 06;	B= fDigit,	Any_Number,	103 ;	N= -3.14
T= 07;	B= fDigit,	Any_Number,	103 ;	N= -3.141
T= 08;	B= fDigit,	Any_Number,	103 ;	N= -3.1415
T= 09;	B= fDigit,	Any_Number,	103 ;	N= -3.14159
T= 10;	B= fSub44,	Subtraction,	501 ;	N=
T= 11;	B= fNeg44,	Negate,	700 ;	N= -
T= 12;	B= fDigit,	Any_Number,	701 ;	N= -2
T= 13;	-B= fDigit,	Any_Number,	701 ;	N= -2
T= 14;	B= fDot59,	One_Period,	702 ;	N= -2.
T= 15;	B= fDigit,	Any_Number,	703 ;	N= -2.1
T= 16;	B= fDigit,	Any_Number,	703 ;	N= -2.14
T= 17;	B= fDigit,	Any_Number,	703 ;	N= -2.141
T= 18;	B= fDigit,	Any_Number,	703 ;	N= -2.1415
T= 19;	B= fDigit,	Any_Number,	703 ;	N= -2.14159
T= 20;	B= fEqual,	Equals,	901 ;	N= -1

***** Closing Trace File *******

Total State Count 20

Appendix B – ITE Trace File

I added a trace to each state to determine how many times a state is entered. The number in the first column is an indication of the order of when a state was entered. My additions to the trace file are indicated by my initial's "gem" in lower-case. The "ready" state at 6, the "begin" at 10, and the "negated1" at 20, etc. were the original positions for tracing state. In the application code, the "begin" state uses a switch with six case statements. If you count the "begin" states below, you will count six state events. This indicates that all six possible transitions were utilized before the negative sign was entered. At the bottom of the trace file, I added the e→sig definitions found in the third column followed by the actual work being done under the column title value. I subtracted the bold states because they get counted twice when the switch uses one of the case statements where there is the original trace.

	State	e→sig	Value
1,	gem-calc,	0	
2,	gem-calc,	0	
3,	gem-calc,	1	
4,	gem-ready,	0	
5,	gem-ready,	2	
6,	**ready**		
7,	gem-ready,	1	
8,	gem-begin,	0	
9,	gem-begin,	2	
10,	**begin**		
11,	gem-begin,	1	
12,	gem-begin,	1107	
13,	gem-negated1,	0,	0
14,	gem-begin,	0	
15,	gem-calc,	0	
16,	gem-begin,	3	
17,	gem-ready,	3	
18,	gem-ready,	0	
19,	gem-negated1,	2,	0
20,	**negated1**		
21,	gem-negated1,	1,	-0
22,	gem-negated1,	1010,	-0
23,	gem-int1,	0,	-3

153

24,	gem-negated1,	0,	-3
25,	gem-Oper1,	0,	-3
26,	gem-calc,	0	
27,	gem-negated1,	3,	-3
28,	gem-Oper1,	2,	-3
29,	Oper1		
30,	gem-int1,	2,	-3
31,	**int1**		
32,	gem-int1,	1,	-3
33,	gem-int1,	1101,	-3
34,	gem-frac1,	0,	-3.
35,	gem-int1,	0,	-3.
36,	gem-int1,	3,	-3.
37,	gem-frac1,	2,	-3.
38,	**frac1**		
39,	gem-frac1,	1,	-3.
40,	gem-frac1,	1010,	-3.
41,	gem-frac1,	1010,	-3.1
42,	gem-frac1,	1010,	-3.14
43,	gem-frac1,	1010,	-3.141
44,	gem-frac1,	1010,	-3.1415
45,	gem-frac1,	1107,	-3.14159
46,	gem-Oper1,	1107,	-3.14159
47,	gem-frac1,	3,	-3.14159
48,	gem-opEntered,	0,	-3.14159
49,	gem-Oper1,	0,	-3.14159
50,	gem-Oper1,	3,	-3.14159
51,	gem-opEntered,	2,	-3.14159
52,	**opEntered**		
53,	gem-opEntered,	1,	-3.14159
54,	gem-opEntered,	1107,	-3.14159
55,	gem-negated2,	0,	0
56,	gem-opEntered,	0,	0
57,	gem-opEntered,	3,	0
58,	gem-negated2,	2,	0
59,	**negated2**		
60,	gem-negated2,	1,	-0
61,	gem-negated2,	1010,	-0
62,	gem-int2,	0,	-2
63,	gem-negated2,	0,	-2
64,	gem-Oper2,	0,	-2
65,	gem-calc,	0	
66,	gem-negated2,	3,	-2
67,	gem-Oper2,	2,	-2
68,	**Oper2**		

69,	gem-int2,	2,	-2
70,	**int2**		
71,	gem-int2,	1,	-2
72,	gem-int2,	1101,	-2
73,	gem-frac2,	0,	-2.
74,	gem-int2,	0,	-2.
75,	gem-int2,	3,	-2.
76,	gem-frac2,	2,	-2.
77,	**frac2**		
78,	gem-frac2,	1,	-2.
79,	gem-frac2,	1010,	-2.
80,	gem-frac2,	1010,	-2.1
81,	gem-frac2,	1010,	-2.14
82,	gem-frac2,	1010,	-2.141
83,	gem-frac2,	1010,	-2.1415
84,	gem-frac2,	1102,	-2.14159
85,	gem-Oper2,	1102,	-2.14159
86,	gem-frac2,	3,	-2.14159
87,	gem-result,	0,	-2.14159
88,	gem-Oper2,	0,	-2.14159
89,	gem-ready,	0,	-2.14159
90,	gem-calc,	0,	-2.14159
91,	gem-Oper2,	3,	-2.14159
92,	gem-ready,	2,	-2.14159
93,	**ready** ,		-2.14159
94,	gem-result,	2,	-2.14159
95,	**result**,		-2.14159
96,	gem-eval,	1104,	-2.14159
97,	gem-result,	1	-1
98,	gem-result,	100	-1
99,	gem-ready,	100	-1
100,	gem-calc,	100	-1
101,	gem-result,	3	-1
102,	gem-ready,	3	-1
103,	gem-final,	0	-1
104,	gem-calc,	0	-1
105,	gem-calc,	3	-1
106,	gem-final,	2	-1
107,	gem-final,	1	-1

e→sig definitions

IDC_1_9	1010	// the numbers one through nine
IDC_POINT	1101	// the decimal point
IDC_EQUAL	1102	// the equal sign
IDC_MINUS	1104	// the negate or minus sign

IDC_OPER   1107   // operand entered
IDC   0
Q_INIT_SIG   1
Q_ENTRY_SIG 2
Q_EXIT_SIG   3

STATE	COUNT	
ITE-States	13	
gem-Calc	10	
gem-Ready	9	
gem-Begin	6	
gem-Negated1	6	
gem-Int1	6	
gem-Oper1	5	
gem-Frac1	10	
gem-OpEntered		6
gem-Negated2	6	
gem-Int2	6	
gem-Oper2	5	
gem-Frac2	10	
gem-Result	5	
gem-Eval	1	
gem-Final	3	
Total 107		

_____ -12 ITE removed because these would be counted twice.
 95 state transitions in the ITE

Efficiency Comparison Temporal vs. Spatial

This matrix shows the number of logic steps compared to the actual work done in the calculator examples.   The work done are these 18 values being entered in the calculator:

-3.14159 - - 2.14159 =

Temporal	Actions (Work)	Logic Steps	Efficiency	Overhead
-pi	8	10	80.0%	20.0%
-pi-(-pi-1)	18	30	60.0%	40.0%
Spatial				
-pi	8	54	14.81%	83.34%
-pi-(-pi-1)	18	96	18.75%	81.25%

The overhead for the Spatial if-then-else explains much of the reason that billions of dollars were lost because of software errors. With 80% of the computer power not going to actual productive work it is surprising that any productive work actually gets done. We all experience this issue when we are working away and the computer decides to take a break for a few seconds then comes back. That is the spaghetti code trying to protect your environment along with helping you get work done all be it at less than 20% efficiency.

The 20% overhead for Temporal can be eliminated, because the Vector can go directly to the action(work) but the code is not as readable.

This page is intentionally left blank so the following images can be compared on opposite pages.

Appendix C – COSA State Diagram

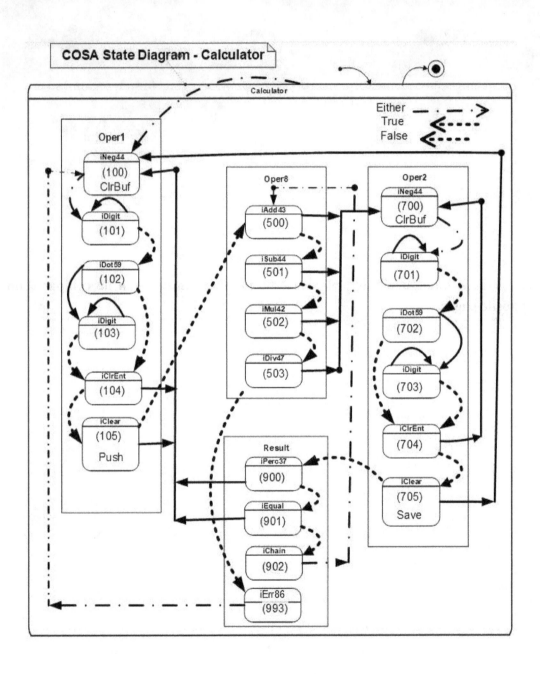

Appendix D – ITE State Diagram

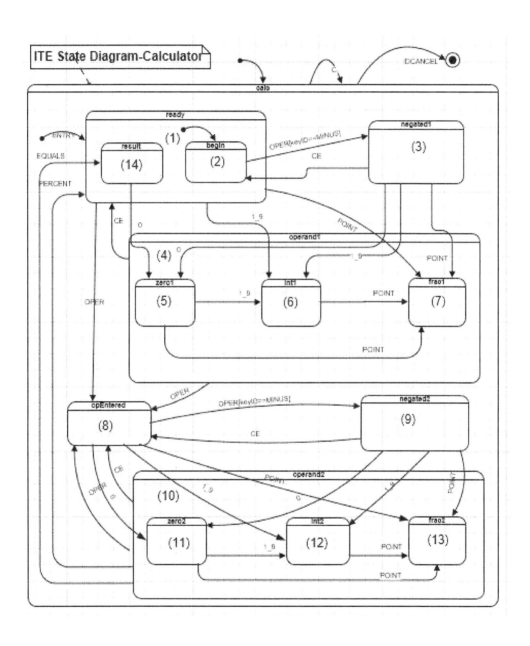

Appendix E – COSA Call Diagram

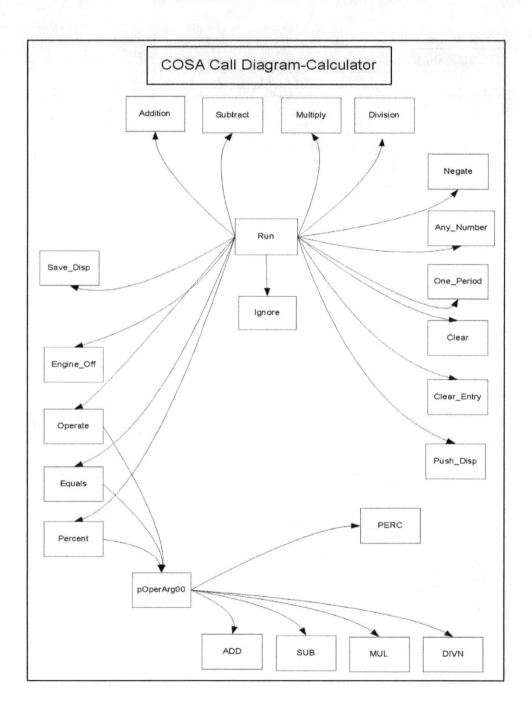

COSA Call Diagram-Calculator

Appendix F – ITE Call Diagram

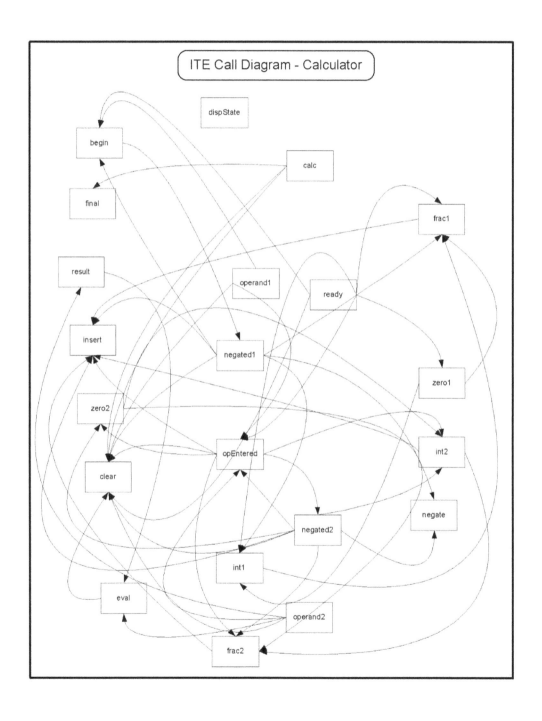

163

Appendix G – COSA Call Trace

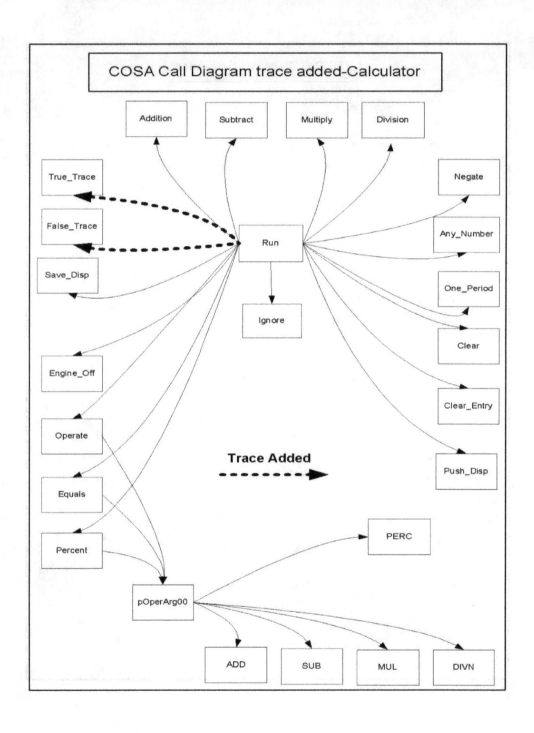

COSA Call Diagram trace added-Calculator

Appendix H – ITE Call Trace

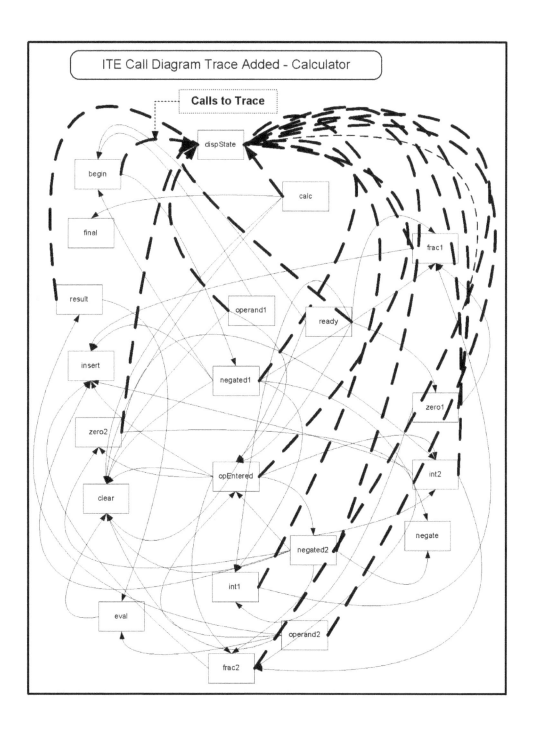

ITE Call Diagram Trace Added - Calculator

Calls to Trace

Appendix I – C++ Calculator Implementation

```cpp
//************* C++ Implementation **********************
void aCalc::Run(int iState, LPCTSTR sDisplay) {
    sNumber = sDisplay;
    engCalc = 1;
    dynamicState = iState;
    while(engCalculate && engCalc){        //Local/Global preemption
      if(dynamicState == Tbl[iTime].state){
              COSA_Trace(iTime);
              (this-*(Tbl[iTime].True_Behavior))();
              iTime = Tbl[iTime].Next_True;
        } else {
              COSA_Trace(-iTime);
              (this-*(Tbl[iTime].False_Behavior))();
              iTime = Tbl[iTime].Next_False;
        }
    }
    pEditWnd-SetWindowText(_T(sBuildNumber));
}
//********************** C++ Implementation **********************
// Calculator Table
struct aCalc::aCalc_Tbl Tbl = {        // statically build rules in table
```

```
//                                      Next                        Next
//                          True        True        False           False
//  Rule      State      Behavior       Rule        Behavior        Rule      Trace
{ca(rOpr1,    iNeg44,  &aCalc::Negate,      rOpr1+,  &aCalc::NotNegate,   rOpr1+,    )},
{ca(rOpr1+,   iAny,    &aCalc::Any_Number,  rOpr1+,  &aCalc::Ignore,      rOpr1+,    )},
{ca(rOpr1+,   iDot59,  &aCalc::One_Period,  rOpr1+,  &aCalc::Ignore,      rOpr1+,    )},
{ca(rOpr1+,   iAny,    &aCalc::Any_Number,  rOpr1+,  &aCalc::Ignore,      rOpr1+,    )},
{ca(rOpr1+,   iClEnt,  &aCalc::Clear_Entry, rOpr1,   &aCalc::Ignore,      rOpr1+,    )},
{ca(rOpr1+,   iClear,  &aCalc::Clear,       rOpr1,   &aCalc::Ignore,      rOpr1+,    )},
{ca(rOpr1+,   iAny,    &aCalc::Push_Disp,   rOpr1,   &aCalc::Push_Disp,   rOpr8,     )},
// operations
{ca(rOpr8,    iAdd43,  &aCalc::Addition,    rOpr2,   &aCalc::Ignore,      rOpr8+,    )},
{ca(rOpr8+,   iSub44,  &aCalc::Subtraction, rOpr2,   &aCalc::Ignore,      rOpr8+,    )},
{ca(rOpr8+,   iMul42,  &aCalc::Multiply,    rOpr2,   &aCalc::Ignore,      rOpr8+,    )},
{ca(rOpr8+,   iDiv47,  &aCalc::Division,    rOpr2,   &aCalc::Ignore,      rOpr2,     )},
// next number
{ca(rOpr2,    iAny,    &aCalc::Engine_Off,  rOpr2+,  &aCalc::Engine_Off,  rOpr2+,    )},
{ca(rOpr2+,   iNeg44,  &aCalc::Negate,      rOpr2+,  &aCalc::NotNegate,   rOpr2+,    )},
{ca(rOpr2+,   iAny,    &aCalc::Any_Number,  rOpr2+,  &aCalc::Ignore,      rOpr2+,    )},
{ca(rOpr2+,   iDot59,  &aCalc::One_Period,  rOpr2+,  &aCalc::Ignore,      rOpr2+,    )},
{ca(rOpr2+,   iAny,    &aCalc::Any_Number,  rOpr2+,  &aCalc::Ignore,      rOpr2+,    )},
{ca(rOpr2+,   iAny,    &aCalc::Save_Disp,   rOpr2+,  &aCalc::Save_Disp,   rOpr2+,    )},
// clear
{ca(rOpr2+,   iClEnt,  &aCalc::Clear_Entry, rOpr2,   &aCalc::Ignore,      rOpr2+,    )},
{ca(rOpr2+,   iClear,  &aCalc::Clear,       rOpr1,   &aCalc::Ignore,      rResu,     )},
// equals
{ca(rResu,    iPer37,  &aCalc::Percent,     rOpr1,   &aCalc::Ignore,      rResu+,    )},
{ca(rResu+,   iEqual,  &aCalc::Equals,      rOpr1,   &aCalc::Ignore,      rResu+,    )},
{ca(rResu+,   iAny,    &aCalc::Operate,     rOpr8,   &aCalc::Operate,     rOpr8,     )},
// error handling
{ca(rErr,     iErr86,  &aCalc::Unknown,     rOpr1,   &aCalc::Error,       rOpr1,     )}
};
```

Appendix I - Matrix

```
//**************** C++ Implementation *********************
        #define ca(r,s,t,nt,f,nf,t) r,s,t,nt,f,nt,t,
```

```
//----------------------------------------------------------------
//Filename           Author          Date              -
//aCalculate.h  Gordon Morrison   23 June 2018          -
//----------------------------------------------------------------


#ifndef aCALCULATE_H
#define aCALCULATE_H
#include "aAReadMe.h"

#include io.h

class aCalc {
public:
// INTERFACE
        aCalc(int iState, LPCTSTR csFilename);
        aCalc();
        ~aCalc();          // normally virtual....
// INTERFACE
private:
        int engCalculate, engCalc;
        int iTime, dynamicState;
```

```
        float    fNumber, fDisplay;
        CWnd *pEditWnd;
        CWnd *pListWnd;
        CStringsBuildNumber, sNumber, sDisplay;
        char    cDisplay32;

public:
        aCalc(CWnd*, CWnd*);
        int      trfl;// trace file
        CStringcsTrcFilename;
        void aCalc::Run(int, LPCTSTR);
        void COSA_Trace(int);
        typedef void (aCalc::*arg0)(void);
        arg0 pOperArg00;
        struct aCalc_Tbl {
                int      ord;
                int      state;
                arg0     True_Behavior;
                int      Next_True;
                arg0     False_Behavior;
                int      Next_False;
                long     rule;
        };

public:
// Calculate Engine Methods because they are initialized in public
  void Error();
  void Ignore();
  void Clear();
  void Clear_Entry();
  void Any_Number();
  void Push_Disp();
  void One_Period();
  void Engine_Off();
  void Save_Disp();
  void Negate();
  void Done();
                void ADD();
                void SUB();
                void MUL();
                void DIVN();
                void PERC();
  void Addition();
  void Subtraction();
  void Multiply();
```

```
  void Division();
  void Percent();
  void Operate();
  void Equals();
  void Unknown();
public:

//*************************************************************
// Insert the following code to user cosa trace!
// NOTE: When DBG is not defined no code is generated in the Engine
//
//#define DBG
//#if defined DBG
//#define xxxxx_Trace(x) COSA_Trace x
//#else
//#define xxxxx_Trace(x)
//#endif
};

#endif


//-------------------------------------------------------------------
//      Filename                Author      Date            -
//      dCalculate.cpp    Gordon Morrison  4 April 18    -
//-------------------------------------------------------------------
#include "stdafx.h"
#include stdio.h
#include fcntl.h
#include stdlib.h
#include io.h
#include sys\stat.h
#include "aCalculate.h"
#include "sCalculate.h"
void aCalc::Error(){
}
void aCalc::Ignore(){
}
void aCalc::Clear(){
        sDisplay.Empty();
        engCalculate = 0;
```

```
            dynamicState = 1;
            sBuildNumber.Empty();
}
void aCalc::Clear_Entry(){
            sDisplay.Empty();
            engCalculate = 0;
            dynamicState = 1;
            sBuildNumber.Empty();
}
void aCalc::Any_Number(){
            sBuildNumber = sBuildNumber + sNumber;
            engCalculate = 0;
}
void aCalc::Push_Disp(){
}
void aCalc::One_Period()
            engCalculate = 0;
            sBuildNumber = sBuildNumber + '.';
}
void aCalc::Engine_Off(){
            engCalculate = 0;
}
void aCalc::Save_Disp(){
            dynamicState = 86;
}
void aCalc::Negate(){
            sBuildNumber = '-';
            engCalculate = 0;
}
void aCalc::Done(){
}
void aCalc::ADD(){
            fNumber = fNumber + fDisplay;
}
void aCalc::SUB(){
            fNumber = fNumber - fDisplay;
```

```
}
void aCalc::MUL(){
        fNumber = fNumber * fDisplay;
}
void aCalc::DIVN(){
        fNumber = fNumber / fDisplay;
}
void aCalc::PERC(){
        fNumber = fNumber * (1.0 + fDisplay/100.0);
}
void aCalc::Addition(){
        pOperArg00 = &aCalc::ADD;
        fNumber = atof(sBuildNumber);
        sBuildNumber = '\0';
        dynamicState = 1;
}
void aCalc::Subtraction(){
        pOperArg00 = &aCalc::SUB;
        fNumber = atof(sBuildNumber);
        sBuildNumber = '\0';
        dynamicState = 1;
}
void aCalc::Multiply(){
        pOperArg00 = &aCalc::MUL;
        fNumber = atof(sBuildNumber);
        sBuildNumber = '\0';
        dynamicState = 1;
}
void aCalc::Division(){
        pOperArg00 = &aCalc::DIVN;
        fNumber = atof(sBuildNumber);
        sBuildNumber = '\0';
        dynamicState = 1;
}
void aCalc::Percent(){
        pOperArg00 = &aCalc::PERC;
```

```
        fDisplay = atof(sBuildNumber);
        sBuildNumber = '\0';
        dynamicState = 1;
        try {
                pOperArg00;
                sprintf(cDisplay,"%g", fNumber);
                sBuildNumber = cDisplay;
        }
        catch (float fNumber) {
                engCalculate = 0;
                dynamicState = 86;
        }
  }
void aCalc::Operate(){
        fDisplay = atof(sBuildNumber);
        sBuildNumber = '\0';
        try {
        (this-*(pOperArg00))();
                sprintf(cDisplay,"%g", fNumber);
                sBuildNumber = cDisplay;
        }
        catch (float fNumber){
                engCalculate = 0;
                dynamicState = 86;
        }
}
void aCalc::Equals(){
        fDisplay = atof(sBuildNumber);
        sBuildNumber = '0';
  try{
                (this-*(pOperArg00))();
                sprintf(cDisplay,"%g", fNumber);
                sBuildNumber = cDisplay;
        }
        catch (float fNumber){
                pEditWnd-SetWindowText(_T("Divide by Zero."));
```

172

```
        dynamicState = 86;
        }
        pOperArg00 = Ignore;
        fNumber = 0.0;
        engCalculate = 0;
}
void aCalc::Unknown(){
}
```

Appendix J

What is a silver bullet?

Before we can define this term there is another term used in the computer industry that may cloud the issue of defining a silver bullet called the "killer app". The software industry is known for claims of a super application ("killer app") that will do everything and pay for itself in very little time. But rarely do these applications turn out to be as good as their claims. Wikipedia defines "killer app" as:

"A killer application (commonly shortened to "killer app") is computer jargon for software which is revolutionary and popular. A killer application may be a video game, web application, desktop application, etc."

Since there are no standard definitions for what constitutes a "killer app". The definition is left up to the market. If a standards committee were to exist for "killer apps" the committee would need to consider the definition by the application's place in time, factoring in marketing hype, a specific market, and the application's popularity within that market.

The silver bullet:

A silver bullet on the other hand is a technology used by technologist. Therefore, its definition will be similar but internal to any application. There are mythical claims that a silver bullet technology will replace existing technologies with vast far-reaching improvements. Wikipedia defines silver bullet as:

"The metaphor of the silver bullet applies to any straightforward solution perceived to have extreme effectiveness. The phrase typically appears with an expectation that some new technology or practice will easily cure a major prevailing problem."

Actually, that sounds rather reasonable like something that should occur on a fairly regular basis. The transistor is an example of a technological silver bullet. The transistor dramatically changed the world we live in. There are many examples of hardware technologies that would be considered silver bullets. But the problem is that these views are with twenty-twenty hindsight. Look at how hardware technology advanced into the super dense integrated circuits. The silver bullet aspect of this technology is taken for granted because Moore's law told us what to expect.

On the software side of computer technology, FORTRAN was clearly a silver bullet over binary and assembly language. But now there is a problem. Software does not have a Moore's law. That is not to say that software has not had impressive gains, because it has. What would a Moore's law for software look like if it existed?

1) The applications would have to decrease in size and increase in performance and reliability.
2) Applications would have to decrease in complexity and increase in features.
3) Applications would have to be easier to trace, debug, and validate as correct.
4) Reuse on all aspects of the engineered software would have to increase.
5) The architecture would have to fit seamlessly into a Model Drive Architecture.

Appendix L – Robot Trace

EA – Elbow Angle; WA – Wrist Angle; FA – Forearm Angle; Trc – Temporal Trace
Target Location – Target X = 250; Target Y = 270

EA = 114.1; WA = 170.9; FA = 148.0; Trc = 1025;
EA = 114.1; WA = 170.1; FA = 135.0; Trc = 1024;
EA = 114.1; WA = 170.1; FA = 135.0; Trc = 1025;
EA = 114.1; WA = 172.2; FA = 130.6; Trc = 1024;
EA = 114.1; WA = 172.2; FA = 130.6; Trc = 1025;
EA = 114.1; WA = 171.5; FA = 119.7; Trc = 1024;
EA = 114.1; WA = 171.5; FA = 119.7; Trc = 1025;
EA = 114.1; WA = 170.5; FA = 104.0; Trc = 1024;
EA = 114.1; WA = 170.5; FA = 104.0; Trc = 1025;
EA = 114.1; WA = 173.3; FA = 96.3; Trc = 1024;
EA = 114.1; WA = 173.3; FA = 96.3; Trc = 1025;
EA = 114.1; WA = 172.4; FA = 83.7; Trc = 1024;
EA = 114.1; WA = 172.4; FA = 83.7; Trc = 1025;
EA = 114.1; WA = 175.6; FA = 79.7; Trc = 1024;
EA = 114.1; WA = 175.6; FA = 79.7; Trc = 1025;
EA = 114.1; WA = 175.2; FA = 74.7; Trc = 1024;
EA = 114.1; WA = 175.2; FA = 74.7; Trc = 1025;

EA = 114.1; WA = 180.0; FA = 67.4; Trc = 1024;
EA = 114.1; WA = 180.0; FA = 67.4; Trc = -1025;
EA = 114.1; WA = 180.0; FA = 67.4; Trc = -1026;
EA = 114.1; WA = 180.0; FA = 67.4; Trc = 1027;

EA = 114.1; WA = 175.2; FA = 74.7; Trc = 1050;
EA = 114.1; WA = 175.2; FA = 74.7; Trc = 1051;
EA = 114.1; WA = 175.2; FA = 74.7; Trc = 1052;
EA = 114.1; WA = 175.2; FA = 74.7; Trc = 1053;
EA = 114.1; WA = 175.2; FA = 74.7; Trc = 1054;
EA = 114.1; WA = 175.2; FA = 74.7; Trc = -1055;

EA = 114.1;   WA = 175.2;   FA = 76.0;   Trc = 1053;
EA = 114.1;   WA = 175.2;   FA = 76.0;   Trc = 1054;
EA = 114.1;   WA = 175.2;   FA = 76.0;   Trc = -1055;

EA = 114.1;   WA = 175.2;   FA = 15.9;   Trc = 1053;
EA = 114.1;   WA = 175.2;   FA = 15.9;   Trc = 1054;
EA = 114.1;   WA = 175.2;   FA = 15.9;   Trc = -1055;
EA = 114.1;   WA = 175.2;   FA = 15.9;   Trc = 1053;
EA = 114.1;   WA = 175.2;   FA = 15.9;   Trc = 1054;
EA = 114.1;   WA = 175.2;   FA = 15.9;   Trc = -1055;

EA = 114.1;   WA = 175.2;   FA = 15.9;   Trc = 1053;
EA = 114.1;   WA = 175.2;   FA = 15.9;   Trc = 1054;
EA = 114.1;   WA = 175.2;   FA = 15.9;   Trc = -1055;

EA = 114.1;   WA = 175.2;   FA =   8.1;   Trc = 1053;
EA = 114.1;   WA = 175.2;   FA =   8.1;   Trc = 1054;
EA = 114.1;   WA = 175.2;   FA =   8.1;   Trc = 1055;
Found Target!

References

The Object-Oriented Thought Process, Matt Weisfeld, Second Edition, Developers Library, Copyright © 2004 Sams Publishing

Practical Statecharts in C/C++, Dr. Miro Samek, Copyright © 2002 CPM Books, www.cpmbooks.com

"Making model-based code generation work," Dr Juha-Pekka Tolvanen, Embedded Systems Europe, August/September 2004, www.embedded.com/europe

Parsing Techniques, Dick Grune, Ceriel J.H. Jacobs, Amstelveen/Amsterdam, July 1990/September 1998

"UML Products by Company," Copyright © 1999-2005 Objects by Design Website

The Mythical Man-Month, Frederick P. Brooks, Jr., Copyright © 1995, Addison-Wesley Publishing Company

Visual Language, Global Communications for the 21st Century, Robert E Horn, Copyright 1998, MacroVu

The Order of Things: How Everything in the World is Organized into Hierarchies, Structures, and Pecking Orders, Barbara Ann Kipfer, Copyright 1998, Random House, Inc.

Open Modeling Language (OML) Reference Manual, Donald Firesmith, Brian Henderson-Sellers, Ian Graham, Copyright 1998, SIGS Reference Library

A Verilog HDL Primer, Second Edition, J. Bhasker, Copyright © 1999, Lucent Technologies

Code Complete Second Edition, Steve McConnell, Copyright © 2004, Microsoft Press.

Index

G

I

M

O

P

R

S

T

www.ingramcontent.com/pod-product-compliance
Lightning Source LLC
Chambersburg PA
CBHW060127060326
40690CB00018B/3786